THE BALANCE OF POWER IN TEST CRICKET

With Best Wishes

Peter Hartland

THE BALANCE OF POWER IN TEST CRICKET

1877 - 1998

Peter Hartland

FIELD PUBLISHING

CROWBOROUGH, EAST SUSSEX

First published in Great Britain by
Field Publishing
17 Tollwood Park
Crowborough
East Sussex
TN6 2XR

British Library Cataloguing in Publication Data.
A catalogue record for this book is available from the British Library.

ISBN 0 9533365 0 6

Design and Typeset by Peter Hartland

Printed by Gwynprint Ltd, Haywards Heath, West Sussex

Peter Hartland is hereby identified as the author of this work in accordance with
Section 77 of the Copyright, Designs and Patents Act 1988

CONTENTS

ACKNOWLEDGEMENT OF ILLUSTRATIONS

Acknowledgement and thanks are given to the following for their kind permission to reproduce photographs of the players listed below:

MCC: Lohmann, Richardson, Barnes, Trumble, Hobbs
Hulton Getty: O'Reilly, Lindwall
Surrey CCC: Bradman, Pollock
Patrick Eagar: Sobers, Richards, Marshall, Ambrose

INTRODUCTION

Do you remember the first cricket history book you ever read? A sea of names, teams, matches, scores and records in some sort of chronological sequence. How long did it take for firm opinions to form? Cricket is the most fully documented of all sports, which is good for those interested in its history because there is access to plenty of information. But what is often lacking is perspective. Even in the area of international Test cricket a clear view of patterns and trends seems to be missing. This is particularly the case if one's contact is limited to the current game because commentators are always citing past players and matches, and overrating them. I remember watching a programme about the remarkable Ashes series of 1981 and Dennis Lillee saying what a great side England were at the time. Lillee is not renowned for generosity towards opponents. That England side had just lost two successive series against West Indies and was about to lose another to India. In the middle of the summer its young captain was discarded and replaced by an old hand who was supposed to have retired. Many of the names bring back fond memories, but of course they were not always at their best and rarely clicked all at the same time. Another distortion is the negative way in which the media positions English cricket of the present day in relation to other countries. The younger followers I have come across tend to focus more on the present. They all assume that South Africa is a traditionally strong cricketing nation and that England is not. In fact South Africa has lost well over twice as many matches against England as she has won.

This book aims to provide some of that missing perspective. It will examine how the nine Test-playing countries have fared against each other through time, both home and away, and identify when the balance of power has shifted in Test cricket, and why. The emphasis rests very much with on-field activity rather than controversy and scandal beyond the boundary. One of the major challenges when writing a cricket book is to say something new. I believe I have done so, but the reader as always will be the ultimate judge. The leading players are assessed more frankly than usual, against fresh statistical analysis broken down by period and concentrating on performance against the strongest opponents. Data is included on the neglected but vital factor of speed of scoring. Too many players from all sports are accepted simply as "great" without sufficient concrete back-up. Taking the adjective, as one should, in its strictest sense, there have been not more than twenty truly great batsmen during the entire history of the game and a similarly small number of really outstanding bowlers. Hardly any have enjoyed a career of uninterrupted success.

A disproportionate amount of cricket history has been written from an English point of view, which has meant that our own players generally loom larger than they should. When John Woodcock selected his 100 Greatest Cricketers for *The Times* in 1997, 40 of them were English, as were nine of the top twelve. Yet in terms of Test results, as we shall see, England ranks fourth behind West Indies, Australia and Pakistan. A few months later another highly respected writer, Brian Glanville, went through a similar exercise for footballers. With many more countries to consider, 34 of his chosen 100 were British. England has won football's World Cup once, less often than five of the other six winners. Yet in Glanville's list, Brazil and Italy were given eleven representatives each, Germany and Argentina five, Uruguay four, and France two.

Part of the problem with cricket history is that far too much importance has been attached to performance in county cricket, whose standards have not approached the highest international levels for a hundred years. Reading about past players, one could sometimes be forgiven for wondering how, with so many geniuses available, England ever lost a match. All our outstanding performers appear to have long retired from the game, most having retired from this life altogether. The anglocentric view of things has also tended to judge overseas teams and players by what they achieved against England, especially in England. There might have been a case for this at one time, but it is certainly inappropriate now.

It will be seen that the balance of power at the highest level of cricket, Test cricket, changes slowly. More slowly than it does in football for example. International football's premier competition, the World Cup, is held every four years, receiving blanket publicity. After France 98, seven countries had won it but only once had the reigning champions retained the trophy. Footballers are at their peak for a shorter time than cricketers. They are required to be fitter, yet are more at risk from injury, and are temperamentally more likely to fall out with manager or teammates. By the time another World Cup comes round, a country's team can be unrecognisable from the last tournament. Moreover, one refereeing blunder can decide the title. *The Times* had this to say shortly after England's footballers' elimination from France 98:

> ...at this level football is a game of luck as well as skill, played and refereed by fallible mortals at almost superhuman speed. The blast of the whistle, the luck of the bounce and the way that the players meet these occupational hazards create its excitement.

Cricket has its own World Cup of course, but only for limited-overs matches. In this form of the game, as in football, the best team does not always win. Test cricket is different. It is, as implied, a proper test: the most fascinating of all contests. Defeating a stronger side over two innings is very difficult, whatever the quality of pitch or umpiring decisions. It is not usual for both teams to lose all their wickets twice, and sporting declarations are more or less unheard of. Winning a series of matches is harder still. Test cricket champions are not easily knocked off their perch, and when it happens, there is a significant reason behind it. There is no official Test cricket championship yet. But, as I hope to demonstrate, it has nearly always been clear who the champions have been.

Peter Hartland
Crowborough
September 1998

1 . PRE-TEST CRICKET AND ITS CHAMPIONS

The origins of cricket, like those of life itself, remain shrouded in a past which history may never fully unravel. For at least a thousand years men, women and children have thrown rounded ball-like objects, hit them with a stick or something similar, and chased after them. Until fairly recently it was thought that a steady evolution down the centuries had produced the game we know today, but research by Peter Wynne-Thomas and Eric Midwinter amongst others indicates that much of this was a combination of wishful thinking and fabrication on the part of early 19th century writers, anxious to preserve the newly-found respectability of formal cricket matches by bestowing on them a longer history than strictly they merited.

The first unequivocal reference to cricket is to a game amongst boys around 1550, near Guildford in Surrey. There are a few references from the 17th century, the most significant relating to a court case at Coxheath near Maidstone in 1646 which involved betting on a game of cricket - the first documented evidence of this. The game must now have been taken seriously.

Organised cricket, by which is meant pre-arranged matches between pre-selected identifiable representative teams, is probably no more than three hundred and fifty years old, and was not a regular occurrence until around 1700. The Association of Cricket Statisticians and Historians lists the first "important" match as taking place in 1707 between Croydon and London in Croydon, and the first "county" game two years later between Kent and Surrey at Dartford. Many clubs today like to make the most of their age, but you are unlikely to see a fixture card quoting a date earlier than these. The first laws were drawn up in 1727.

Cricket was born in the southern English counties of Hampshire, Sussex, Surrey and Kent, and it is here that it first developed into a recognised sport. During the first two-thirds of the eighteenth century the strongest teams tended to lie within, or take the name of, Kent, though the 1730s and 1740s saw Sussex, in particular the village of Slindon, establish superiority, while at other times Surrey, with its draw on London, defeated all-comers.

Around the mid-1760s the balance of power moved to Hambledon, just over the Hampshire border with Sussex. There the game was first intellectualised, rendered professional, its standards raised to a marked degree. Until then the bowler had simply rolled the ball along the ground, but now the idea of allowing it to bounce just once before reaching the batsman - pitching - took hold. This enabled the game to move faster because both bowler and batsman gained an advantage: the former in effectiveness of underarm delivery, the latter in range of strokeplay. John Small senior, Hambledon's first leading batsman and the first to reach three figures on the ground, developed the straight bat defensive technique. Scoring levels increased. Gerald Brodribb has calculated that during the fifty years to 1770 the average was around 7.5 runs per wicket, or 75 all out. By the turn of the nineteenth century it had reached double figures.

With people not travelling much at this time, the distinction between village and county teams was very hazy. The romantic story passed down is that of a tiny remote village, Hambledon, defeating the might of England, time and again. In fact Hambledon was primarily a club which organised fixtures on its ground. The team based there was usually called "Hampshire" although it sometimes secured the services of leading players from over the county border, then renaming itself "Hambledon", and even lent its own men to the opposition. The "England" team was generally drawn from the remaining players from the other three counties: Sussex, Surrey and Kent.

The Hampshire club held sway for much of the remainder of the eighteenth century, until the game's power base moved to London and Lord's, headquarters of the Marylebone Cricket Club, or MCC as it is better known. London, or "Surrey", cricket was strongest during the first two decades of the nineteenth century but it was a period when little cricket was played due to the Napoleonic Wars. When the game resumed in earnest many bowlers, whose arms had been creeping higher anyway, began delivering from around shoulder level, though the law did not accept "roundarm" bowling until 1835.

The county as a cricketing unit became more established in the mid-1820s. Peter Wynne-Thomas has drawn up a list of unofficial county champions during years when this is possible. He begins in 1826, when the champions are Sussex, who retain their title the following year before giving way to Kent in 1828. Wynne-Thomas names champions for only three of the next eight years, Surrey winning twice and Sussex once. Kent then take three titles on the trot from 1837 to 1839 and another hat-trick in 1841-43. This was the famous side of Felix, Wenman, Hillyer, Pilch and

Mynn, with whom a contemporary poem stated "'twas but natural to win". Kent and Sussex share the honours during the latter half of the 1840s, before the re-emergence of Surrey during the following decade, and the arrival of the first strong northern county, Nottinghamshire. Yorkshire does not come to the fore until the end of the 1860s. The county championship was only officially constituted in 1890, the first universally accepted points system having been introduced two years previously. Before then, opinions differed on which county, if any, should be placed above the rest, though during the two decades prior to the championship being formalised few disputed that the most accomplished county was Nottinghamshire.

Interest in county matches was variable. There was a decline following the forming in 1846 of William Clarke's powerful All-England Eleven to spread cricket throughout the land. Within three years it was easily the strongest side in the country, even if most of its fixtures were with local sides against odds. From 1849 to 1856 the most keenly contested fixture of the year was North versus South, the Northern team winning eight matches to their opponents' four with one drawn. In 1857 the All-England Eleven began playing a breakaway United All-England Eleven, and this became the highlight of the season for the next few years, honours remaining more or less even.

All these matches held more attraction than the MCC showcase, Gentlemen versus Players, first staged in 1806. The problem with this fixture was that for a long time the Gentlemen were unable to give their professional opponents a decent game. All kinds of ruses were tried to even things up: given men; extra men; even a different size wicket. Sixty years later the Gentlemen found the answer: a young man by the name of WG Grace.

To place Grace in perspective it is necessary for a moment to forget the popular image of the portly greybeard. Picture him instead in 1873 as a 25 year-old, already noted for prodigious feats in track and field athletics. At this stage he had scored more runs in his short cricketing career - over 10,000 - than anyone else in history to date, at more than double the average. His career average was now 61, the next best that had been achieved being Richard Daft's 29. Grace was literally twice as good as anyone who had ever played, and if he had retired there and then, his average would still be higher today than any other Englishman's. With a step-change in broad-batted technique, if not in style, he was the first to show that cricket could be a batsman's game; that bowlers could be forced on the defensive for long periods. The important thing to remember about Grace is not so much his cricketing longevity, remarkable though that was, but the fact that he established a lead over his contemporaries which has never been equalled.

Grace was the first great cricketer, but the hundred years between underarm "pitching" and the legalisation of overarm bowling in 1864 produced a number of other significant players whom it is worth pausing to identify. The most accurate of the early pitchers was 'Lumpy' Stevens. Then David Harris demonstrated just what could be achieved with underarm bowling. Harris was not only accurate, but generated significant pace and lift from the pitch by jerking the ball out from under the armpit. He could not have kept a straight arm. Harris's bowling produced more catches than others, but no one knows how many. Until the mid-1830s bowlers were not credited with wickets unless the ball hit the stumps.

It is easier to compile figures for the batsmen. William Beldham of Surrey started out in the Hambledon era, carrying on well into the 19th century, and was acknowledged the most accomplished player of underarm bowling. In the major matches I have managed to locate, he scored over seven thousand runs at an average of 21. He also fathered 39 children. Stonewaller Tom Walker was aptly named, according to a contemporary, because his slowness between the wickets led to his being frequently run out. He still managed an average of 19. The two best players to establish themselves around the turn of the nineteenth century were Lord Frederick Beauclerk, average 24, and William Lambert, with an impressive 27. Both were also good bowlers. To counter increasing scoring, more and more bowlers in the 1820s and 1830s followed the trend of delivering with a higher arm, and it worked. In 1810 the average runs per wicket in what the Association of Cricket Statisticians and Historians class "important" matches was 13; in 1820 the same. By 1830 it had dropped to 10, and by 1840 to 9. In 1850 a slight recovery had brought the level back to 11. Fuller Pilch, generally regarded as the best batsman to this time, scored 7147 runs between 1820 and 1854 at an average of 18. His studious left-handed teammate, Felix, finished with the same average while making just over half the number of runs. Pilch and Felix appear to compare unfavourably with Lambert, but they were up against more difficult bowling and also defended a larger wicket.

Roundarm bowlers reaped a rich harvest. The most successful was accurate medium-pacer William Lillywhite of Sussex, a contemporary of Pilch, who took over 1500 wickets. The best fast bowler was John 'Foghorn' Jackson, in the 1850s and 1860s, so called because blew his nose every time he took a wicket. Jackson moved the ball both ways and was thought to be comparable in pace to the swiftest full overarmers forty years on. WG Grace considered George Freeman of Yorkshire to be the finest fast bowler he faced, and that was early in Grace's career when he was at his most dominant. The most famous performer from the pre-Grace era was the much-loved all-rounder Alfred Mynn, a gentle giant of a fast bowler, big hitter and safe slip catcher, who at one time weighed in at 24 stone.

While bowlers' arms climbed progressively higher until the law recognised the inevitable in 1864, there was no comparable advance in batsmanship. This was because pitches, still rough and ready with scant regard for evenness or slope, had barely improved. The only tool in regular use was the scythe, complementing the work of rabbits, sheep and, on one reported occasion at Lord's, a brace of partridges. So little preparation was involved, in fact, that choice of pitch was normally left until the morning of the match. As long ago as 1788 the Laws had made provision for cutting, rolling and covering - sweeping was added later - but much of this was theory rather than practice.

The heavy roller became available around the time Grace scored the first 2,000 runs in a season in 1871, by when runs per wicket had risen to 17 in English first-class cricket. A decade later it was being used in tandem with the grass mower over tended soil, the groundsman's job having extended beyond keeping trespassers at bay, and being now recognised as something approaching an art. By the last decade of the nineteenth century, average scoring levels in England had reached the mid-twenties. There they remained for fully ninety years before extended covering of pitches in the 1980s pushed the figure over the thirty mark.

When the Test match era began in 1877, the process of allowing the batsman as fair a chance as the bowler, though reasonably well advanced, still had a way to go. And the idea of an undisputed champion team was at best only half-formed. It took international cricket to bring it into the public consciousness.

2 . OVERVIEW OF TEST MATCH RESULTS

Before embarking on the chronological detail of Test cricket, and in order to present it in context, a broad perspective of overall Test match results may be useful. The clearest way to view the nine Test-playing nations in an order of merit is to concentrate on those matches which yielded a positive result. In other words to remove draws and ties from the equation. Over 60% of Test matches have produced a winner, and the proportion is increasing. The following table gives the percentage of each country's wins from matches they either won or lost: at home; away; and overall.

Percentage Test Wins from Matches with Positive Results (ignoring draws and ties)

		Home	*Away*	*Total*
1	West Indies	71	55	**61**
2	Australia	65	53	**60**
3	Pakistan	78	40	**56**
4	England	61	48	**54**
5	South Africa	45	32	**39**
6	India	55	17	**36**
7	Sri Lanka	48	13	**27**
8	New Zealand	36	18	**26**
9	Zimbabwe	20	0	**7**
Total		59%	41%	**50%**

includes all matches to 31 August 1998

Home teams win 59% of Tests with positive results, the equivalent of a 3-2 series victory. The table shows the countries in terms of four pairings, with new boys Zimbabwe adrift at the bottom. West Indies are in front with a ratio slightly in excess of three wins for every two defeats. Australia follow close behind. Pakistan and England, the two other countries with more wins than losses, vie for third place. A large gap separates them from South Africa and India, who in turn are some way ahead of Sri Lanka and New Zealand.

Pakistan is the most formidable home side, with over three wins for every defeat. There have been a lot of draws in Pakistan though, and the most difficult place to avoid defeat, as opposed to win, has been the Caribbean. The difference between the Indians' home and away form is remarkable. They are over three times as effective at home. With a smaller sample size, the Sri Lankans are nearly four times as likely to win on their native island.

The table overleaf indicates how the teams have fared against each of their opponents, home and away. All have met, apart from Zimbabwe not having yet played Australia or West Indies. We are again interested only in matches won and lost. This time countries are shown in the order they began playing Test cricket.

West Indies and Australia have the best of everyone at home, including each other. In contests between the top two, Australia is six games up. West Indies are ahead in England, New Zealand and India, but behind in Pakistan and level in Sri Lanka where they have played just one, drawn, Test. The Australians have not travelled as comfortably as one might expect, except to South Africa. They are well down in Pakistan and surprisingly level in New Zealand. In England they are one game to the good. England at home dominates New Zealand, India and South Africa, and has lost out only to West Indies and by that one match to Australia. Elsewhere the English are in credit only in New Zealand and South Africa. The Pakistanis' strength on their own pitches is confirmed, the one blot on their copybook being a recent blip against South Africa. Their morale has suffered when visiting the more established teams.

South Africa has a lot of ground to make up on England and Australia, and has only just begun to tackle the non-white countries. India and New Zealand appear rather a pushover abroad, though the latter is level in Sri Lanka. The Indians have been a match for anyone at home – apart from West Indies – and the improving Sri Lankans, as mentioned, are another side from the sub-continent to show a strong preference for their own pitches. Zimbabwe have won just the one game so far, but for them it is early days.

17

Total Test Wins and Losses: by Country and Opponents Home and Away									
Home Team									
	Eng	Aus	SA	WI	NZ	Ind	Pak	SL	Zimb
	W L	W L	W L	W L	W L	W L	W L	W L	W L
England	*	40-41	24-7	18-28	21-2	22-3	13-7	2-1	-
Australia	73-52	*	14-5	25-18	10-2	16-3	12-4	5-0	-
South Africa	14-25	9-18	*	-	8-3	3-0	2-1	2-0	-
West Indies	23-10	11-10	1-0	*	3-0	14-2	8-3	1-0	-
New Zealand	2-15	5-5	0-4	4-7	*	4-4	3-6	4-1	2-0
India	11-10	8-9	2-1	5-14	9-2	*	4-2	6-0	1-0
Pakistan	2-1	7-2	0-1	7-4	12-2	5-0	*	6-2	3-0
Sri Lanka	1-1	0-2	0-1	0-0	3-3	1-1	1-3	*	4-0
Zimbabwe	0-0	-	0-1	-	0-0	0-0	1-3	0-0	*
Neutral Venue (England) – Australia 2 South Africa 0									
includes all matches to 31 August 1998									

The next table shows the world's leading team, as I see it, at the end of each calendar year. Where a series is in progress as the new year comes in, it is ignored unless the result has already been decided. As noted earlier, there has rarely been any doubt about the identity of the unofficial champions.

18

The Evolving Balance of Power in Test Cricket

World's Leading Team 1877-1997

Period	Leading Team	Years Reign
1877-78	England	2
1879	Australia	1
1880-81	England	2
1882-83	Australia	2
1884-91	England	8
1892	Australia	1
1893-97	England	5
1898-1903	Australia	6
1904-07	England	4
1908-11	Australia	4
1912-20	England	9
1921-25	Australia	5
1926-29	England	4
1930-32	Australia	3
1933	England	1
1934-52	Australia	19
1953-58	England	6
1959-64	Australia	6
1965-67	West Indies	3
1968-74	South Africa	7
1975-76	Australia	2
1977	England	1
1978	West Indies	1
1979	England	1
1980-94	West Indies	15
1995-97	Australia	3

Total Years at Top

Australia	52
England	43
West Indies	19
South Africa	7
Total	**121**

England and Australia have been playing Test cricket against each other for 121 years, and for much of that time were far stronger than any other country. Whoever held The Ashes were effectively world champions. This is evident when looking chronologically at their respective Test results against the other nations. It took 58 years for England to lose a home series against anyone other than Australia, South Africa winning here one-nil in 1935, and a further fifteen before West Indies recorded their first success in England. On both these occasions the victors were hammered by Australia soon afterwards, proving they still had some way to go to reach the top.

Home advantage was particularly important for England because she made no attempt to send her strongest side anywhere other than Australia until 1930, apart from one tour to South Africa on the eve of the First World War. From 1930 to the early 1950s, English touring sides were only representative to Australasia and South Africa. The other countries could only properly test their relative strength against England, in England. Before the First World War, even Australia was in this position, albeit to a lesser extent. Not one of the fourteen English touring parties to play Tests in Australia during this period contained the best possible team. Leading amateurs, generally our better batsmen, could rarely spare the time, and tours were privately organised, their teams privately selected, until MCC took responsibility in 1903. England and Australia could only meet at full strength in the Mother Country, and then only when the Australians did not leave some of their best players behind, which they did as a result of internal disputes in the latter half of the 1880s and in 1912.

Australia remained unbeaten in any series, home or away, by countries other than England for 79 years, until 1956 and a solitary defeat on the mat in Pakistan. The Aussies' first home series defeat against other opponents came 103 years after their first Test Match – in 1980 against West Indies. The first time the leading team in the world was neither England nor Australia was in 1965, when West Indies' defeat of Australia followed a comfortable win in England. Two years later South Africa had also beaten both Australia and England, and could claim soon afterwards to be undisputed world champions as both their vanquished foes beat West Indies.

The South Africans were certainly the strongest side when they were excommunicated from international cricket at the beginning of the 1970s, and it took a while for a crystal clear successor to emerge. Australia rose to the top under Ian Chappell in the middle of the decade, before losing her grip in the wake of the Packer Revolution. England were the short-term beneficiaries, before West Indies assumed the mantle. After one Packer-assisted slip which allowed England back in for a year, West Indies ruled the roost throughout the whole of the 1980s and half the 1990s. They were finally overthrown by the Australians, who have been champions for the past three years.

By my reckoning only four of the nine Test-playing countries have held the unofficial championship: Australia, England, West Indies and South Africa. Pakistan's results overall are much better than South Africa's, but Pakistan has not sustained a peak long enough to reach the top.

3 . EARLY TEST CRICKET (1877-1893)

World's Leading Team 1877-1893

Period	Leading Team	Years Reign
1877-78	England	2
1879	Australia	1
1880-81	England	2
1882-83	Australia	2
1884-91	England	8
1892	Australia	1
1893	England	1

The first international cricket match was actually between USA and Canada in 1844, and the first English overseas tour was to North America in 1859. Then came the American Civil War, which nipped in the bud the development of the game on the East Coast. In 1861-62 an English party travelled instead to Australia, and the rest is history.

The first eleven-a-side international contests – Test matches – which took place in Australia in 1877 did not raise much interest in England. Even after the sides won a match apiece, and Charles Bannerman scored the first Test century for the home team, the widespread view, challenged only by the players who had toured, was that proper cricket was played in the Mother Country and nowhere else. The Australians' tour to England the following year changed all that.

The 1864 law giving bowlers the freedom to deliver above shoulder height – overarm – was seen at the time as confirmation of what was already happening, but few English bowlers had taken full advantage by the end of the following decade. WG Grace's assault on the wild slingers had encouraged a philosophy of containment on a line of off-stump and outside, led by Alfred Shaw of Nottinghamshire, the only man in history to deliver more overs than have runs taken from him. Shaw was a canny operator who dismissed Grace no fewer than 49 times. When he bowled the first ball in Test cricket in 1877, his hand was above the shoulder on delivery, but the action was still nearer roundarm. It was the Australian bowlers, particularly Spofforth, who demonstrated to a stunned English public just what could be achieved with a genuine overarm action and a more direct, aggressive approach. The ball kicked more steeply and ripped off the pitch faster, while the higher arm brought also a natural sideways movement into the stumps (as opposed to the roundarmer's "twist" to leg), which often found the customary gap between bat and pad. The more vertical delivery of full overarm was also easier to aim accurately than roundarm, as brief experimentation will prove. To subject the batsman to even more pressure, a new position of silly-mid-on was introduced, and behind the stumps spectators had never seen anything like the wicket-keeping of Blackham, with his skill at standing up to quickish bowling without the protection of a long-stop.

The 1878 Australians played no Tests, winning seven and losing four of their fifteen first-class fixtures. But for the first time they came up against pretty well the full strength of England – an MCC eleven at Lord's. What followed was nothing short of a sensation, MCC being bundled out twice for totals of 33 and 19, and beaten by nine wickets – all within a single day. Spofforth took ten wickets for 20 in the match, Boyle nine for 19. Punch published a poem:

> The Australians came down like a wolf on the fold,
> The Marylebone cracks for a trifle were bowled,
> Our Grace before dinner was very soon done,
> And Grace after dinner did not get a run.

It was from this point that English cricket began to think international. The fact that the Australians established themselves so quickly as a serious threat ensured the elevated status of England v Australia matches.

At the turn of the following year a team of English amateurs, bolstered by two professional Yorkshiremen Ulyett and Emmett, took on an Australian XI in Melbourne in what was subsequently known as the third Test match. The English assumed they had the batting to win but finished up being beaten by ten wickets, Spofforth taking thirteen for 110. The margin of the Australians' victory made it difficult to dispute their superiority. A truer test of the countries' relative strengths came in 1880 at The Oval, when England for the first time fielded a fully-representative side in a formal international fixture. WG Grace made his Test debut at the age of 32 and scored 152 in England's first innings, as the home team won by five wickets. On this occasion Australia could claim to have been weakened, for Spofforth was missing injured.

Australia grabbed back the imaginary crown by winning two matches against an all-professional touring line-up in 1881-82, when Ulyett was easily the most successful batsman, then emerged victorious from the famous Oval Test of 1882. This last game might not have caused quite the same shock at the time as the defeat of MCC four years earlier, but it has passed down in folklore because the beaten side was England, and because it led to the story of The Ashes. England were set 84 runs to win in the last innings on a rain-affected wicket, and despite Grace's 32 were dismissed seven short. This time Spofforth was playing and took seven wickets in each innings. The following winter England regained "The Ashes" by winning two of three pre-arranged matches in Australia, but a fourth was won by the home side, levelling the series.

England won the three-match home rubber in 1884, courtesy of an innings victory at Lord's. But the Australians had the better of the two drawn games, Murdoch making 211 at The Oval. This match gave evidence of the depth of English batting when Walter Read made a hundred at number ten. That winter, an all-professional side visited Australia. The Australians were entering an era of internal disputes and selection difficulties which would weaken them for the remainder of the decade, while English cricket was stronger than ever. England won the first two games of the series before the home side demonstrated familiar fighting qualities to draw level. In the decisive match at Melbourne, a Shrewsbury hundred set up a comfortable win for the tourists.

Shrewsbury's 164 not out in nearly seven hours at Lord's in 1886 was one of the greatest bad-wicket innings ever played. England won all three Tests that year. Briggs took 11 wickets at Lord's; Lohmann 12 at The Oval where Grace hammered 170 out of 216 while he was at the crease. Between 1887 and 1890 there were eight Tests, only one of which was contested on a decent wicket. Taking full advantage of rain-affected surfaces was an integral part of the game at this time, and a right-arm/left-arm combination could produce convenient footmarks. The Australians now had Turner and Ferris, or 'Terror' and 'Fiend' as they were dubbed by a media engrossed by Jack The Ripper; the English Lohmann and Peel, though the latter usually delivered from round the wicket. These four wrought absolute havoc. In seven of the eight games, England's stronger batting carried her through – a rare period of batting, rather than bowling, winning Test matches.

The first of two games in Sydney in 1887 saw England dismissed in the first innings for 45, which remains her lowest ever Test score (Mike Atherton's men managed one more in Trinidad 107 years later), but Shrewsbury's team still managed to win by 13 runs! Turner and Ferris shared 17 wickets. They bagged 18 in the following game and were again on the losing side, Lohmann returning match figures of 10 for 87 for the tourists.

In early 1888 two separate English parties were in Australia, and they combined to play a one-off Test, again at Sydney. On another treacherous surface, Turner took 12 for 87 for the home side; Peel 10 for 58 and Lohmann 9 for 52 for the visitors. The decisive contribution was Shrewsbury's opening 44, the highest score of the match and worth a big hundred in other circumstances. Back in England later that year the Australians began with a 61-run win at Lord's, Turner and Ferris sharing 18 wickets while skittling the home team out for 53 and 62. Grace's second innings 24 was the top score on either side. England won the remaining two games by an innings. The Oval provided a welcome true pitch, but Old Trafford was another gluepot. Grace again made the game's highest score, 38, and Peel took 11 for 68. There were two Tests in England in 1890. The home team won the first by seven wickets, Grace's 75 not out once more being top knock; and the second more closely by two wickets.

The Australian cricketing public had become disillusioned by their teams being defeated time after time, and by the self-damaging internal politics. They could not take much more. Australia's 2-1 home victory in 1892 was thus important, particularly since WG Grace himself led a strong English team. His previous visit to the country had been eighteen years earlier, before Test cricket had begun. Australia won the first two games, not entirely convincingly, thirteen wickets going to both Turner and George Giffen, who was back after a five-year absence. But it is the result that counts, and England's innings win in Adelaide could not wipe the smile from Australian faces. England were a more formidable side at home in 1893, and won the three-match rubber 1-0. Shrewsbury, who had missed the recent tour, produced another of his masterly wet-wicket efforts (106) at Lord's to thwart the rampaging Turner, receiving positive support from Jackson (91) on debut. At The Oval Jackson made 103 not out in 135 minutes before Briggs and Lockwood secured an innings victory. An injury to Lockwood enabled his Surrey fast bowling partner Richardson to make a first appearance at Old Trafford. Richardson typically marked the occasion with ten wickets.

Considering the ardous nature of travel over land and sea at the time, enthusiasm must have been high for these tours to follow one another at such a breathtaking rate. The early games were generally a battle between England's clearly superior batting and the sharper outcricket of the Australians. When England's bowling caught up with Australia's in the mid-1880s there was a procession of English victories both home and away (seven series wins in succession from 1884 to 1890) before the Australians to their considerable relief emerged victorious at home in 1892. The introduction of marl in England during the 1880s, together with the increased use of heavy roller and mower, rendered pitches truer, reducing the chances of the underdog – provided it did not rain. By 1893, when she quickly regained The Ashes, England had won ten matches at home and lost only two. In Australia better batting surfaces, and better batsmen, came during the 1890s with Bulli and Merri Merri Creek soils. The score Down Under up to 1893 reads a more even ten victories apiece.

In the next table it will be seen that of those men who played most of their international cricket between 1877 and 1893, and scored 850 runs in England v Australia Tests, only three managed averages over thirty. Australia's best bat was Billy Murdoch, who possessed the stamina for the big score and registered the first Test double century, but looked uncomfortable on a sticky surface. Arthur Shrewsbury, rather slow and the first consciously to use his pads as a second line of defence, was the acknowledged expert on bad wickets, and this frequently proved decisive, most notably at Lord's in 1886. Broadly speaking, the worse the pitch, the greater the relative influence on the match of batsmen over bowlers. Shrewsbury contributed as much towards winning, as opposed to saving, Test matches as any single batsmen has ever done. Grace too was still a formidable player and influence, even if his best days had been back in pre-international times.

Averages remain the best single measure of cricketing performance – and the fewer measures we are confronted with, the clearer the picture – but taken at face value they can be misleading. The nature of pitches, and levels of scoring, have changed as the game has evolved, which means that it is not a lot of use comparing the averages of players from different generations. It makes more sense to restrict initial statistical comparison to groups of players within the same set period, when conditions were broadly similar, and then to include only their performances against the stronger opponents. I will be doing this for each period to the present day. Data is taken from appropriate matches during a player's entire career, not just during the era in question. For batsmen the measures are average runs scored per dismissal, and scoring rate in terms of runs per hour. The latter measure is taken from batsmen's innings of 100 or more in the Test matches stipulated. In some cases the sample size will be small, but when a man makes a hundred there is time for the real character of his play to come out. In the rare instances where a batsman made no hundred, the scoring rate is taken from his highest innings. Time is preferred to balls faced, mainly because there is a lot more data available, but also because it takes into account the important ability to manipulate the strike. Today's slower over rates obviously affect comparison of players from different eras, but not players from the same era. With the minimum run qualifications in place, these two measures are sufficient to identify the leading batsmen of the period. The higher each figure, the better it reflects on the batsman. A lot of nonsense is talked about the supposed significance of how often a player reaches a hundred. In itself, incidence of hundreds is not a very meaningful measure. It is the average which counts. Three eighties are a lot more use than a hundred and two ducks.

To indicate general levels of scoring, the Average Runs per Wicket is given for the selected matches within each era. For bowlers, a line will be drawn to show who took their wickets at an average better, and worse, than the general rate. Specialist batsmen are expected to return an average above normal in order to compensate for their less-able colleagues. For them the line is drawn at a point one and a third times the Average Runs per Wicket (e.g. for an Average Runs per Wicket of 30 the batting line would be drawn at 40). Those on par for their period appear sandwiched between two lines.

The first of these tables show players who featured mainly between 1877 and 1893, and cover only Tests between England and Australia. South Africa's first Tests against England in 1889 are not included. The South African teams in the two matches were of barely first-class strength, while the English tourists fielded only four men who had appeared at home against Australia the previous summer, and two who actually made their only first-class appearances during the series. The English side won the first Test by 8 wickets, and the second by an innings and 202 runs after dismissing their opponents for 47 and 43. Briggs achieved match figures of 15 for 28!

It is common to find faster scorers lower down the averages, the risks they take rendering them less consistent. One of the true measures of greatness in a batsman is a high average and a quick scoring rate. It will be seen that Grace stands out here. For a hitter McDonnell's average is pretty respectable. Alec Bannerman's rate of of 12 runs per hour is the lowest to be found anywhere in my tables. It is based on one innings of 94 but is typical of his stonewalling style. The over-rate in those days was brisk, and Bannerman must be a strong candidate for the slowest batsman of all time.

Averages of Batsmen who featured mainly between 1877 and 1893

Matches included: *All Tests between England and Australia.*
Average Runs per Wicket = *20*   *x **1.33** = 26*
Qualification: *850 runs*

	Average	Runs per Hour
Shrewsbury (Eng)	35	22
Grace WG (Eng)	32	38
Murdoch (Aus)	32	26
McDonnell (Aus)	28	38
Ulyett (Eng)	25	37
Giffen (Aus)	23	38
Bannerman AC (Aus)	23	12

To assess properly the impact and effectiveness of bowlers, a measure of wickets per match is needed to complement the traditional average of runs conceded per wicket taken. The traditional average is the product of Strike Rate (wickets taken per hundred balls) and Economy Rate (runs conceded per hundred balls), divided by one hundred, and thus covers the effect of both. The best bowlers should have a high wickets per match ratio and a low bowling average. For the first bowling table the qualification is 50 wickets.

Reading contemporary accounts it is not always easy to categorise the following bowlers. All apparently used "break" yet only Bates, a roundarmer, is consistently referred to as a slow bowler. Finger-spin was a principal weapon of them all, but those who tended to push the ball through were often classed as medium-pacers. Today, only Spofforth would be considered fast-medium, and probably only Turner and Palmer medium-fast.

HS Altham's *History of Cricket*, first published in 1926, drew on first-hand sources and included this revealing description of Lohmann's bowling:

> subtlety of flight was his greatest asset; with his very high delivery he was always dipping short of what the batsman expected; he could suck him out with his held-back slow ball, or get him driving at the half-volley which somehow 'swam' on into a yorker.

Lohmann has always been regarded as a medium pacer, but spin must have produced that deceptive flight. He enjoys a clear lead in these averages, but the Australians, remember, were up against better batsmen. Lohmann was also by some way the most successful bowler of his time in domestic cricket, which meant rather more in those days than it does now.

Averages of Bowlers who featured mainly between 1877 and 1893

Matches included: All Tests between England and Australia.
Average Runs per Wicket = 20
Qualification: 50 wickets

	Type	Average	Wickets Per Match
Lohmann (Eng)	RM	13	5.1
Barnes W (Eng)	RM	15	2.4
Turner (Aus)	RMF	16	5.9
Peel (Eng)	SLA	16	5.1
Bates (Eng)	LB	16	3.3
Spofforth (Aus)	RFM	18	5.2
Briggs (Eng)	SLA	20	3.1
Palmer (Aus)	RMF	21	4.5
Giffen (Aus)	OB	27	3.3
Notable non-qualifier:			
[Ferris (Aus)	LM	14	6.0]

Key to bowling types: RFM = Right arm fast-medium; RMF = Right arm medium-fast; RM =Right arm medium pace; LM = Left arm medium pace; LB = Leg-break; OB = Off-break; SLA = Slow left arm orthodox

On rain-affected or under-prepared pitches, of which there were plenty, Turner, who could place an orange between his first two fingers and squeeze it to pulp, was the most destructive of the lot with his sharp break back into the right-handed batsman. This reflects in a very high 5.9 wickets per Test. He still holds two unbeatable records in first-class cricket: the only instance of 100 wickets in an Australian season, and the highest number of wickets (283) by a tourist during a single English summer. On a true surface the subtler variation of Spofforth and Lohmann was more feared, particularly their barely discernible change of pace. Peel, especially, and Briggs took full advantage of their opponents' lack of experience against orthodox slow left-arm on turning wickets. This would become a traditional English weapon. Peel was a firm believer in unwavering length, a message passed on from his respected Yorkshire predecessor Peate, who gave the ball more air but less spin from a highish roundarm action. Briggs preferred to mix it up, exercising less control. George Giffen's figures reveal that, for all his feats in non-international first-class cricket, he was not quite the outstanding all-rounder at the highest level that his reputation would suggest. From the start the Australian bowlers were supported more athletically and reliably in the field, as they nearly always have been, with their wicket-keeper Blackham in a class of his own.

4 . THE GOLDEN AGE (1894-1914)

World's Leading Team 1894-1918

Period	Leading Team	Years Reign
1894-97	England	4
1898-1903	Australia	6
1904-07	England	4
1908-11	Australia	4
1912-18	England	7

The twenty years before the First World War are known as The Golden Age of Cricket. This is largely because pitches had improved, but not too much, and the balance between bat and ball was about right. In England cricket was at its highest level of popularity relative to other sports, notably football. Another reason is that England and Australia were more evenly matched than at any time. In the more representative matches in England, which were often rain-affected and low-scoring, the home side shows a narrow 7-6 lead over the period, with Australia 17-13 ahead Down Under. Matches in England were still limited to three days, while those in Australia were played to a finish.

England with a little luck emerged victorious from two pulsating closely-fought series in 1894-95 and 1896. In the first rubber, the opening Test in Sydney saw the visitors follow on yet still contrive to win by 10 runs. They won the next match at Melbourne after being dismissed for a first innings 75. Australia enjoyed easy victories in the next two Tests, generating massive public interest in the fifth, deciding, game, which England won by six wickets. Richardson, magnificent and tireless, bagged 32 wickets and Peel 27 for the tourists, while for Australia George Giffen at last stamped his all-round authority on a series. The following year in England, after one win apiece the third and last match was decided as much as anything by the weather. Richardson again shone, with 24 wickets in the first two Tests, getting through 110 overs at Old Trafford where the Indian prince Ranjitsinhji marked his debut with 62 and a scintillating 154 not out. This was the match England lost!

Australia established herself as the undisputed leading cricketing power by winning four successive series between 1897-98 and 1902, two decisively in Australia and two narrowly in England where her opponents were at full strength – or should have been had the selectors known what they were doing. The key Australians during this five-year period were Clem Hill, a high-class left-handed batsman, strong against fast bowling, who has always been rated higher in his own country than in England where the softer wickets were not always to his liking; Hugh Trumble, tall off-spinner of just below medium pace with a shrewd brain and deceptive flight; and Monty Noble, a genuine all-rounder: sound bat, resourceful bowler mixing quickish off-spin with a new outswerve, fine close fielder, and subsequently one of Australia's most astute captains, who introduced the idea of pre-planned fields for individual batsmen with inner and outer rings to prevent both singles and boundaries. Shock tactics were provided by Ernest Jones, the fastest bowler seen to that time and, in response to easier pitches, the first to bounce batsmen regularly.

Australia's series win in 1899 was only their second in England, after 1882, and resulted from the tourists winning the only game to be decided, by ten wickets at Lord's. Hill and a young Victor Trumper made hundreds and Jones took ten wickets. The 1902 series is often considered the zenith of the Golden Age, even though it was one of the wettest English summers. The weather prevented a result both in the first Test, which England would have won, and the second. Australia comfortably won the third at Sheffield in dreadful smoke-filled light, the one and only Test ever played there. Hill scored another important century after Trumper had demoralised the bowling at the start of the second innings. Noble captured eleven wickets.

The dramatic final two games emphasised how little there was to choose between the cricketing strength of the two countries at the time. Both times Australia won a good toss. Trumper hit a hundred before lunch on the first day of the fourth Test at Old Trafford. Jackson's 128 in reply was made in more difficult conditions, and as the wicket deteriorated further the home side was left 124 to win in the last innings against two of the bowlers best equipped to exploit it. Trumble and left-arm spinner Saunders bowled the visitors to victory by just three runs to clinch the series. At The Oval, England's last innings target was a lot more formidable – 263 on if anything an even worse wicket. At 48 for 5 even the most partisan of the 18,000 home supporters had given up. What then happened has passed into legend,

Gilbert Jessop showing that his amazing 80 runs per hour hitting in county cricket – two and a half times the average rate according to Gerald Brodribb's research – could be transferred, if tantalisingly seldom, into the sterner international arena. "The Croucher's" 104 took a mere hour and a quarter. Trumble bowled from one end throughout the match to finish with 12-173 and was accorded a modicum of respect, but the rest of the attack, as so often said about Jessop on the rampage, was reduced to the level of the village green. What made Jessop a formidable batsman, albeit a highly unorthodox one, as opposed to a slogger was his quick footwork. He could play straight – though this quite often meant straight back over the bowler's head – and no tutor could fault his rasping square cut. But he probably gained more satisfaction from pulling the good length ball high over the leg side (it is possible the term "cow shot" may first have been applied to him) or from slicing it over extra cover. Jessop's heroics at The Oval created the possibility of a miraculous win but others had still to contribute. Fortunately three doughty Yorkshiremen answered the call. Jackson played a vital supporting role early on, then Hirst, also enjoying his best game for his country with top-score and five wickets in the first innings, guided England home by one wicket with Wilfred Rhodes.

South African cricket made strides during this period but could not produce a national eleven to match the best of England or Australia. Development was hampered by all important games in the country being played on matting. In 1896 a second scratch English side went out to play three Tests. George Lohmann was already in South Africa recovering his health, and once he joined the touring party any possibility of an even contest disappeared. Lohmann's respective match figures were 15 for 45 (including 8-7), 12 for 72 (including 9-28) and 8 for 87. Needless to say, all three games were won easily. Three years later another unrepresentative English touring team won the two Tests staged. The South Africans' batting and bowling were still way below international standard, but they did have a superb wicket-keeper in Halliwell.

Australia's first tour to South Africa in 1902 was an important catalyst for improvement there. The Australians were on their way back from England so had most of their big names on view. South Africa achieved her first draw, before going down in the remaining two Tests. England visited again in 1906, with only three of the men who had helped retain The Ashes the year before, and paid for her complacency. Sticking sensibly to the same eleven players throughout the five-match series, South Africa swept to a 4-1 triumph. There was a first sight of the four googly bowlers, who had refined Bosanquet's discovery, and captain Percy Sherwell was another excellent wicket-keeper. Such an impression did they make that the South Africans were invited for a three-Test series in England in 1907: their first chance against a true England eleven. In a wet summer they gave a good account of themselves, losing the one Test to be decided by 53 runs at Leeds when Blythe's left arm spin claimed 15 wickets for 99. But the English did not heed the lesson, and travelled to South Africa in 1910 with only Blythe of their best bowlers, then only picked him for the last two Tests. In the final match he took ten wickets. England lost the rubber 3-2, her most successful bowler being Simpson-Hayward with underarm lobs. Two of the googly practitioners, Vogler and Faulkner, shared 65 wickets and Faulkner also made over five hundred runs.

South Africa's first visit to Australia in 1910-11 was a personal triumph for Faulkner, who this time topped seven hundred runs in the Tests. His bowling made little impact, however, and only Schwarz with 25 wickets adapted his wrist-spin successfully to Australian conditions. The visitors lost four Tests, but did at least notch their first genuine Test win, by 38 runs at Adelaide, despite Victor Trumper making 214 not out. The Triangular Tournament, staged in the drenched English summer of 1912, confirmed that South Africa still had some way to go to match the big two, losing five Tests and drawing the other. Three meetings with Sydney Barnes yielded that formidable character 34 wickets, and worse was to come.

When England deigned to send something nearer to a full side to South Africa in 1913-14, she proved far too strong, winning four Tests and drawing one. Barnes found the matting very much to his liking, taking ten wickets at Durban, seventeen at Johannesburg, eight during the return match at Johannesburg and fourteen at Durban again. Feeling that he had exerted himself sufficiently in his country's cause, he sat out the final game. By the outbreak of the First World War the South Africans' progress had been visible, but they remained prone to being found out by the very greatest players. Lohmann demolished them in 1896 (35 wickets in three matches at an average of 5); Barnes between 1912 and 1914 (83 wickets in seven matches at an average of 9). Trumper averaged 94 with the bat against them in 1910-11, while Jack Hobbs had secured over a thousand Test runs from South African bowling by the time war was declared.

The qualification for the next set of averages takes in South Africans' Test efforts against Australia, and against England in England. South African performances against English touring sides are excluded, apart from that last series before the war. English and Australian performance against South Africa still does not count. The following players appeared mainly between 1894 and 1914, but not afterwards. Figures for the likes of Rhodes and Armstrong, who carried on after the war, therefore come later. The batting qualification for English and Australian batsmen increases to 900 runs.

Averages of Batsmen who featured mainly between 1894 and 1914 and did not appear afterwards

Matches included: All Tests between England and Australia. For South Africans: performance in all Tests against Australia; all Tests against England in England; Tests against England in South Africa 1913-14.
Average Runs per Wicket (England v Australia Tests) = 27 x 1.33 = 36
Qualification: 900 runs for English and Australian batsmen;
800 runs for South Africans

	Average	*Runs per Hour*
Jackson (Eng)	48	34
Ranjitsinhji (Eng)	44	48
Hill (Aus)	35	38
Stoddart (Eng)	35	33
Hayward (Eng)	35	30
MacLaren (Eng)	33	31
Trumper (Aus)	32	40
Duff (Aus)	32	37
Darling (Aus)	30	40
Tyldesley JT (Eng)	30	32
Noble (Aus)	30	27
Gregory SE (Aus)	25	44
Trott GHS (Aus)	21	40
Notable non-qualifiers:		
[Fry (Eng)	31	40]
[Jessop (Eng)	24	81]

Jackson never visited Australia, where runs at this time were easier to come by, and even for a Yorkshireman his confidence and capacity to rise to the big occasion were remarkable. More of a stylist than most from his neck of the woods, Jackson's career average of 33 in all first-class cricket was around the norm for the period. The batting star of the Golden Age in England was Ranjitsinhji, with a first-class average of 56 – virtually as high as any English-qualified player has ever achieved and quite phenomenal for the time, particularly since he scored at around 50 runs an hour. Taking a qualification of ten thousand runs for all English batsmen who faced their first ball in the nineteenth century, Ranji's first-class average is approached only by Sussex teammate Fry with 50. Only two others managed an average of forty: Tom Hayward jr (41) and Johnny Tyldesley (40). The table indicates that Test bowling did not slow Ranjitsinhji down much, and the combination of his high average and scoring rate in relation to the others really does mark him as out of the ordinary. The sight of this slight, dark figure working the fastest bowling calmly to the leg-side boundary struck onlookers as some kind of oriental conjuring trick. Excluding Ranji, and noting that Fry and Jessop do not make the table, the Australians apart from Noble now score much faster than their opponents.

The greatest of them was Victor Trumper. Trumper's form waxed and waned in rough correlation with his health, and his figures as generally reported do not stand out as exceptional. But they are actually quite impressive when taken, as they should be, alongside those of contemporaries. In Ashes Tests his average is respectable enough, and by 1914 no one had equalled his six hundreds. Moreover, no Australian retiring by this juncture had matched his first-class average of 44. Where Trumper remains unapproached to this day is in the range and grace of his strokeplay, and in his ability to carry on attacking successfully with those strokes on pitches so treacherous that others were grateful merely to survive. The perceptive Noble commented:

> You had to be in with him to realise his ability to the full. The most difficult and dangerous strokes were made with consummate ease. His action was so free, in fact, that onlookers were often deceived into the belief that he was facing the easiest of bowling.

Trumper scored even faster than Ranji in first-class cricket in England, at a rate of 56 runs per hour. To place him in context, one can say that there has never been a greater batsman for a three-day match on a bad wicket.

The belated realisation that nothing less than the strongest available English team was now required prompted MCC to take over tour organisation and selection from 1903. Two series successes immediately followed to put England back on top. The triumph in 1903-04 by the odd match in five owed much to Rhodes' 31 wickets – still the most ever taken by an English slow bowler in a rubber in Australia. But for dropped catches it would have been several more. Victor Trumper scored 574 runs but complained that Rhodes never gave him a moment's peace. In the first match RE Foster, another gifted amateur with plenty of other things to do, rattled up 287, the highest Test score to date. In 1905 England enjoyed her most comfortable home series of the period, her batsmen completely mastering the tourists' attack, which had now lost Trumble.

Most of England's best batsmen stayed at home in 1907-08, some feeling they had not been offered enough money, and Australia won by four Tests to one. The key bowler was Saunders who had missed the 1905 trip. The depth of English bowling at this time was illustrated by the success of "reserves" Crawford and Fielder, who took 55 wickets between them in support of Sydney Barnes. Rhodes' bowling had lost much of its effectiveness, but he kept his place for all five Tests, wrongly, on the strength of his developing batting. Colin Blythe appeared in just one Test, despite the fact that he was now the best slow bowler in England and would remain so until the suspension of first-class cricket in 1914. A competent violinist, Blythe demonstrated a wider repetoire than Rhodes, including a deadly inswinging quicker ball which came from nowhere. Ranjitsinhji for one rated him highest among bowlers of this type. With Rhodes they said that every ball looked the same, but wasn't. The one thing Blythe lacked was the Yorkshireman's equanimity. An epilectic, he worked himself into such a state during big games that a doctor once forbade him to play for England at Lord's. Blythe's appearances in the most important matches were nevertheless more limited than they should have been.

The Aussies won a low-scoring series here in 1909 by making more of their resources. England's greater strength in depth proved to be her undoing as the divided selectors could not decide what was their best side and kept chopping and changing. Blythe and Hirst bowled the home team to a ten-wicket win in the first match at Edgbaston, which prompted the victors to make five changes. Not surprisingly the initiative was lost. Second innings collapses against Armstrong at Lord's, and Cotter and Macartney at Leeds decided the issue. In the drawn fifth Test at The Oval, Bardsley became the first batsman to score a hundred in each innings of a Test match.

Lancastrian captain Archie MacLaren and selector Lord Hawke of Yorkshire departed the England scene after this series. Their running feud had blighted selection ever since Hawke refused to release Hirst and Rhodes for the 1901-02 trip to Australia under MacLaren. The latter summoned Sydney Barnes from the leagues as a replacement, receiving plaudits for his judgement as Barnes bowled well in Australia. Another row led to both Hirst and Barnes being dropped for the 1902 Old Trafford Test, the one England lost by three runs. Hirst was actually left out on the morning of the game. Hirst reappeared famously at The Oval, but not Barnes. The following year, after only two seasons with Lancashire, Barnes walked out of county cricket for ever. For him it was a simple question of economics. The leagues paid him more money for less work. Such an attitude elicited little sympathy from the England selectors, who ignored him for another four years. It was all right for amateurs such as Jackson and Fry to please themselves when they turned out for county and country, but the likes of Barnes, a working-class professional, were expected to know their place. He was recalled only when England struggled to get a side together for the 1907-08 Australian tour, bagging 24 wickets while demonstrating what the Australians had suspected all along: that he was the best bowler in the world. In 1909, however, he was stupidly left out of the first two Tests, returning to take 17 wickets in the last three. It is quite probable that with sensible selection England would have reversed the results of both the 1902 and 1909 series.

Barnes has more often than anyone else been called the greatest of all bowlers, in this country at least, and the abnormal size of his hands had something to do with it. His method was unique in that his stock ball was spun out of the front of the hand at above medium pace and turned from leg. It was virtually indistinguishable from the one that went, more naturally for most people, the other way. Because Barnes powerfully spun, rather than cut, every ball, he produced spin-swerve in the opposite direction to break, and extracted abnormal bounce. He also delivered very few loose balls. The Australians, as noted, always rated him on their wickets. On South Africa's mats he was well nigh unplayable. Had he been invited there in 1910, England would have turned defeat into victory. Perhaps too in 1906. Barnes's decision to give up county cricket to dominate the leagues, where he captured 4069 wickets at 6.08 runs apiece, kept him fresh and made him a more formidable bowler at Test level – a lesson perhaps for our present day administrators.

The next table gives the figures of the most successful Golden Age bowlers against the best batsmen. Trumble leads the averages. His 141 wickets in Ashes Tests remained a record until the 1980s and still no one has matched his two hat-tricks. Historians, particularly English ones, have been apt to underestimate his impact. Saunders shows a higher wickets per match ratio than might be expected. More reliant than some on a helpful pitch, he should certainly have been picked in 1905. Australia has five men here to England's two. Those two are the greatest bowlers we have ever produced from the fast and medium-fast categories.

Averages of Bowlers who featured mainly between 1894 and 1914 and did not appear afterwards

Matches included: All Tests between England and Australia. For South Africans: performance in all Tests against Australia; all Tests against England in England; Tests against England in South Africa 1913-14.

Average Runs per Wicket (England v Australia Tests) = 27
Qualification: 50 wickets for English and Australian bowlers;
                40 wickets for South Africans

	Type	*Average*	*Wickets Per Match*
Trumble (Aus)	OB	20	4.5
Barnes SF (Eng)	RMF	21	5.3
Noble (Aus)	RM	24	2.9
Richardson (Eng)	RF	25	6.2
Saunders (Aus)	SLA	25	5.3
Cotter (Aus)	RF	28	4.1
Llewellyn (SA)	SLA	28	3.3
Jones (Aus)	RF	29	3.3
Notable non-qualifiers:			
[Lockwood (Eng)	RF	20	3.5]
[Blythe (Eng)	SLA	21	4.5]

Key to bowling types: RF = Right arm fast; RMF = Right arm medium-fast; RM = Right arm medium pace; OB = Off-break; SLA = Slow left arm orthodox

Tom Richardson's strengths were consistency and stamina. He could bowl virtually all day without any noticeable let-up in pace or desire. Richardson did not employ the variation of his Surrey and England partner Lockwood, and generally stuck to a full length, bringing the ball back prodigiously off the pitch from a glorious side-on action. Unlike most fast bowlers, Richardson was not easily ruffled, judging correctly that he was good enough to bowl sides out without resorting to intimidation. He generally operated with only two men on the leg side, one of whom was at fine-leg to collect inside edges. Richardson's 6.2 wickets per match is the highest ratio in any of my tables, and he was also responsible for an achievement unapproached in the entire history of fast bowling: 1005 first-class wickets in just four English summers. He is one of only three English bowlers to have taken 20 wickets in a series in Australia twice, the others being Barnes and Peel – all before the First World War.

Peel's record against Australia is as good as any English left-arm spinner's, but he was operating at a time of helpful pitches before the Australian batting had fully developed. One of the weaknesses of finger-spin, left-arm orthodox or off-break, is that it generally relies on drying, dusty or underprepared wickets for success. On true firm surfaces, most finger spinners are reduced to trying to keep the runs down and waiting for a mistake. As an attacking force on good wickets, the most effective English orthodox left-arm spinners have been those with the capacity and intelligence to make the most deceptive use of flight: Rhodes and Blythe. They were Golden Age contemporaries and rivals for a place in the England team, one reason why Rhodes after a few years turned his attention to batting. Rhodes the bowler was at his peak for half a dozen years from the time he first appeared against Australia in 1899. A master of subtle variation, with the psychological shrewdness to go with it.

Rhodes' record as an all-rounder will be seen in the next set of tables to be very similar to Noble's. The difference is that the Australian's batting and bowling peaks coincided, whereas Rhodes was more or less finished as a Test match-winning bowler with a quarter of a century of his international career still to run, despite ending up with more first-class wickets than anyone in history. By the time of England's 1911-12 trip to Australia he was opening his country's batting with Jack Hobbs, one of two decisive partnerships which rendered this probably England's strongest ever touring side. At Melbourne they put on 323 together. The other pairing was that of Barnes, at 38 a regular choice for the first time, with Frank Foster. Foster bowled left arm medium-fast from round the wicket, swinging into the body and moving it the other way off the pitch at some pace. On mostly perfect batting pitches, this was the only time two English bowlers have each taken thirty wickets in a series in Australia.

England defeated her hosts by four matches to one, but the side was still considered in need of bolstering with a couple of amateur batsmen, Fry and Spooner, for the return matches a few months later. Fry at last was made captain. He is one of several famous names from the period who did not impress at the highest level – that is against Australia – to the extent one might assume, until looking carefully at the figures. Others who do not qualify for the tables given here include Hirst and Jessop, both of whose fondness for the pull shot led them to come unstuck on faster Australian pitches, where Hirst's bowling was also pretty harmless. The reputations of all three men are built largely on achievement in domestic cricket, not forgetting Jessop's one stupendous Test hundred, and the same can be said of bowlers Lockwood and Blythe. All are legends, but none significantly affected the balance of power in international cricket.

With fewer opportunities, the qualification in the tables for South African cricketers is slightly lower: 800 runs for batsmen and 40 wickets for bowlers. It may be a surprise to see left-arm spinner Llewellyn as the South Africans' sole representative, and none of their four googly bowlers, who were the first to bring this method under control and employ it as a regular means of attack. Many of their wickets, however, came in matches against far from representative English touring sides, which have been excluded from the reckoning here. Schwarz delivered nothing but googlies, but was the only one to make any impression in Australia. The most complete bowler of the four was Vogler, a killer on matting, though some found Faulkner just as difficult to pick. Gordon White, the remaining member of the quartet, was more of a batsman.

Between 1912 and 1914 England's superiority was really made to count – in Australia; at home during the Triangular Tournament against the South Africans and an Australian team weakened by internal dispute; and then in South Africa. When the nineteenth century, which had effectively begun in 1815 with Napoleon's defeat at Waterloo, came to its real end in 1914, English cricket was stronger than ever.

5 . BATSMEN'S PARADISE (1920-1949)

World's Leading Team 1919-49

Period	Leading Team	Years Reign
1919-20	England	2
1921-25	Australia	5
1926-29	England	4
1930-32	Australia	3
1933	England	1
1934-49	Australia	16

We have already seen that before 1914 England only ever fielded her strongest possible team at home. Of the thirteen home series against Australia to this time, England had won nine to Australia's four, and all four Australian victories had been by the odd game. Immediately before the First World War England had been dominant. This goes some way towards explaining the profound impact made in 1921 by Warwick Armstrong's Australians, which is evident in much defeatist writing since. A five-nil loss in Australia the previous winter was an unwelcome first, but there had been three four-one reverses there before, and as far as many English followers were concerned the real test was in England. After three games the result of that test was clear, as all three were won by Australia with embarassing ease. The last two matches were drawn. There had obviously been a major shift in the balance of power. Australia for the first time were streets ahead.

What had happened? Nine years had elapsed since the teams had last met, and it seemed a lot longer. Of course there had been a devastating war, but one in which the Australians had also played their part. The war had claimed not only a million lives from the British Empire, but also much of the energy, confidence and optimism of the period before. In 1921 people were already looking back to a Golden Age which could never return. They still are.

On paper there was nothing wrong with England's batting, which actually appeared stronger than their opponents'. The batsmen who were to become the four leading first-class runscorers of all time – Hobbs, Woolley, Hendren and Mead – were all on the scene, although the most important one, Hobbs, missed much of the season through injury and illness. The crucial difference lay in the bowling, where England no longer had a genuine Test-class performer and Australia had three. Barnes was 47 when he effectively turned down a place on the 1920-21 tour to Australia, by insisting that his wife accompany him as a paid guest. His powers had scarcely diminished, and if he was not asked the following summer, he should have been. Foster had suffered a permanent wartime leg injury; Rhodes, despite renewed success with the ball for Yorkshire, was no longer a force at the highest level; Tate's miraculous transformation from innocuous county off-spinner into one of the legendary medium-pacers was a couple of years away. Blythe was dead, killed on the Somme, and had anyhow retired in 1914. In a dry summer there was no opportunity for one of our remaining finger-spinners to catch the Aussies on a rain-affected wicket. As before, the selectors constantly shuffled the team around, which only reinforced the impression of a rout.

It took more than forty years for a Test captain to consider seriously a tactic which is now second nature: opening the bowling with two fast bowlers. They decided the series. Jack Gregory, with bounding run, giant leap and a liberal dose of bouncers, was the more intimidating. Ted McDonald approached softly, before a beautifully smooth action propelled the ball at generally fuller length with movement either way. Bert Oldfield, one of the greatest and most stylish of wicket-keepers, was in a perfect position to observe them:

> Gregory, to my mind, always swung the ball much more effectively than his team-mate and he was, if anything, slightly faster while the sheen remained on the ball. Once the newness was worn off he relied entirely on pace, whereas McDonald was able to turn the ball back from the off even at his fastest speed, and with this ball could be most destructive. The spin which McDonald imparted added speed to his delivery in a most deceptive manner, after the ball made contact with the pitch. On the other hand, Gregory's delivery did not gain pace from the pitch, rather did it lose impetus, particularly on a lifeless wicket.

Oldfield had no doubt that McDonald was the better bowler, though he was unsuccessful both in the previous rubber in Australia and the one after in South Africa. These three series represented the entirety of McDonald's Test career, for he then settled in England, throwing in his lot with Lancashire. A third member of the attack was Arthur Mailey, who applied prodigious spin to his leg-breaks and googlies without bothering too much about length or giving away runs. A few months earlier he had taken 36 wickets in the four Tests in which he had bowled. In support, Armstrong the captain offered up an altogether different type of leg-spin, delivered curiously between thumb and second finger: very tight, at times blatantly negative. He averaged only 1.7 wickets per match against England. Armstrong was not supposed to have a googly, but a rare clip of film taken at The Oval in 1921 clearly shows him bowling somebody with one. He was a better batsman than he looked, particularly after filling out in middle age, and invariably had to be dug out. In overall first-class cricket his record is formidable. Utilising the method of dividing career batting average by bowling average to derive an all-round ratio, Armstrong (46 over 19 = 2.42) is the most successful all-rounder of all time.

His side were also far ahead of their opponents in the field. Every member of England's team at Leeds was over 30 years of age, the only instance of this in Test history. The one reason above all responsible for the massive Australian superiority was the fact that Australia's cricketers, brought up in a hot climate and youthful, outdoors culture, mature far more quickly than their English counterparts. They found it much easier to hit the ground running after a long break denying vital years of development. Exactly the same thing happened after the Second World War.

The Average Runs per Wicket for the next table is taken from the four Ashes series either side of the Great War – eight in all. This table highlights more clearly than traditional statistics the two outstanding batsmen from the generation whose Test careers straddled the confict. Charlie Macartney began as a slow left arm bowler before concentrating his attention on batting. The combination of his average and scoring rate is impressive, like Grace and Ranjitsinhji previously. No top-class batsman got away with so many improvised risks. Like many small men he was very quick on his feet, with strong flexible wrists. One of the best descriptions compared him to a rackets player hitting winners from all over the court. Nottinghamshire would have seen what was meant by this when he made 345 against them in under four hours. For Macartney, dominating the bowler was just as important as making a big score, and he loved to whip straight balls through the leg side. In many ways he was the nearest of the old-timers to Vivian Richards.

Averages of Batsmen whose Test Careers straddled the First World War

Matches included: All Tests between England and Australia. For South Africans: perfomance in all Tests against Australia; all Tests against England in England; Tests against England in South Africa 1913-14 and from 1930.
Average Runs per Wicket (England v Australia Tests 1907-26) = 31 x 1.33 = 41
Qualification: 1000 runs for English and Australian batsmen; 900 runs for South Africans

	Average	*Runs per Hour*
Hobbs (Eng)	54	32
Macartney (Aus)	43	41
Faulkner (SA)	41	32
Taylor (SA)	37	35
Armstrong (Aus)	35	35
Woolley (Eng)	33	42
Bardsley (Aus)	33	33
Rhodes (Eng)	31	27
Nourse sr (SA)	28	29

Jack Hobbs, a genius of a different kind, holds a big lead in these averages. Before the war he played a more dashing game, in keeping with the spirit of the age and his own youthful instincts, but his batting was always based on sound orthodoxy and perfect technique. Hobbs remains one of the two greatest English-born batsmen – Grace is the other – his position resting on an ability to master all types of bowling on any wicket, turf or matting. More than any other batsman in history can it be claimed that he had no weakness. As EW Swanton said:

> Of all batsmen he was the most versatile; the glazed wickets of Sydney and Adelaide, the matting of Johannesburg and Durban only enhanced his reputation.

The more difficult the circumstances, and the greater the pressure, the more likely was Hobbs to make a hundred, without taking all day over it.

Contemporary with Hobbs over a long career, Frank Woolley is still the standard by which all elegant left-handers are judged. Many words have been written about the effortless beauty of his play, the long reach and full swing sending the ball skimming to, or over, the boundary. Fast bowlers frequently posted a long-off. Perhaps there was something a little too loose about his batting – more so even than the man from a later generation most often compared with him, David Gower. Woolley's record, bearing in mind the high-scoring 1920s, is no more than satisfactory, despite what enchanted writers such as the normally sober Swanton might say. He also took two thousand first-class wickets with left-arm spinners, but was not really a Test bowler unless the pitch was turning. Australian opener Warren Bardsley was another left-hander. He was more comfortable in English conditions than against the best English bowlers on his own soil, where Barnes, Foster and Tate all troubled him.

The man who came nearest to conquering the mighty Barnes was the South African Herbie Taylor – on the mats in 1913-14 when none of his teammates had a clue. Here he explains how:

> I played Barnes the way I did those magnificent googly bowlers Vogler, Schwarz, Faulkner and White when I came into first-class cricket. I kept my eyes glued to the ball in his hand as he ran up to the wicket. And just before he delivered it I would switch my eyes to about a yard above his head to catch any finger movement as the ball left his hand. It was no use picking up the ball after it had left the hand of a bowler like Barnes because you would have no idea of what it would do off the pitch. Once I knew what sort of delivery it was going to be it was a case of forward to the ball you can meet and back to the ball you can't. Of course, you have to be quick with your footwork but what I have told you now is the really very simple secret of batting.

With his decisive footwork and orthodox technique, Taylor was sometimes likened to Hobbs. He always looked good, but was not relatively as effective on turf as on the matting surfaces South Africans were brought up on. Taylor averaged 50 in first-class cricket in South Africa; a more modest 34 on grass pitches elsewhere. Aubrey Faulkner makes the table largely on account of his prolific series in Australia in 1910-11. He scored few runs in England.

Faulkner does not appear in the following rather small bowling table, but two other leg-spinners do. Pegler bowled the occasional off-break for variation but no googly. He was one of the successes of the Triangular Tournament but was not considered much use on matting, being selected for only one home Test. Rhodes' average is good but 2.6 wickets per match is not very impressive for a bowler with his reputation. In mid-career he was regarded more or less as a specialist batsman.

Averages of Bowlers whose Test Careers straddled the First World War

Matches included: All Tests between England and Australia. For South Africans: performance in all Tests against Australia; all Tests against England in England; Tests against England in South Africa 1913-14 and from 1930.

Average Runs per Wicket (England v Australia Tests 1907-26) = 31

Qualification: 50 wickets for English and Australian bowlers; 40 wickets for South Africans

	Type	Average	Wickets Per Match
Rhodes (Eng)	SLA	24	2.6
Armstrong (Aus)	LBG	30	1.7
Pegler (SA)	LB	33	3.0

Key to bowling types: LBG = Leg-break and googly; LB = Leg-break; SLA = Slow left arm orthodox

The three decades from the end of the First World War to the century's halfway mark were the easiest in the history of the game in which to score runs. One run scored then was worth nearly two made in the 1880s. Lord Hawke reckoned that a club side of the 1920s would have turned their noses up at being asked to play on some of the first-class wickets of forty years earlier. Pitches were now over-prepared, particularly in Test matches, rendering all but the best bowlers powerless unless it rained and an uncovered surface allowed swift revenge. The ultimate torture for hapless trundlers came during timeless Tests under a burning southern hemisphere sun. Australian wickets were rock hard and virtually grassless, removing any shine from a new ball within a few overs. Between the wars Australia had the better of England overall, winning 22 Test matches to 15, and six series to three. English touring teams were now more or less at full-strength in Australia, if not elsewhere, and England's record there was actually better than at home. The high points were the decisive 4-1 wins in 1928-29, when Hammond amassed nine hundred runs, and 1932-33, the controversial Bodyline tour. But perhaps more satisfying after three series under the cosh was the recovery of The Ashes at The Oval in 1926. On a damaged second-innings pitch Jack Hobbs made 100 in good time, his finest innings, supported as so often by trusty opening partner Herbert Sutcliffe, who finished with 161. The Australians were polished off by Wilfred Rhodes, recalled to the colours at the age of 48.

Averages of Batsmen who featured mainly between 1920 and 1949

Matches included: All Tests between England and Australia. All Tests between England/Australia and South Africa from 1935. For players from other countries: performance in all Tests against Australia; all Tests against England in England; all Tests against South Africa from 1935. For South Africans: also performance against English touring team 1930-31. For New Zealanders: also performance in Tests against English teams returning from Australia. *Average Runs per Wicket (England v Australia Tests) = 36* x *1.33 = 48*

Qualification: 1500 runs for English, Australian and South African batsmen; 900 runs for the rest

	Average	Runs per Hour
Bradman (Aus)	89	36
Sutcliffe (Eng)	64	24
Leyland (Eng)	57	31
Hammond (Eng)	56	29
Nourse jr (SA)	53	31
McCabe (Aus)	52	45
Headley (WI)	49	28
Mitchell (SA)	48	24
Ponsford (Aus)	47	32
Woodfull (Aus)	44	25
Rowan EAB (SA)	43	24
Hendren (Eng)	39	33
Notable non-qualifier:		
[Merchant (Ind)	47	25]

Sutcliffe is the highest-ranking Englishman in the batting table for the epoch. He and left-handed fellow-Yorkshireman Leyland were tough fighters, never giving an inch while making the utmost of their ability, which in each case was self-acquired rather than naturally endowed. Wally Hammond, with greater gifts, was a wonderful stylist off either front or back foot. There has been no more majestic driver through the off-side. He was more successful against the Australians on their own pitches, taking his time through matches with no limit. At home he was not always happy against wrist-spinners O'Reilly and Grimmett, particularly when they concentrated on his leg-stump. Interestingly because it was never commented upon at the time, EW Swanton has also recently suggested an unease against fast bowling, citing Hammond's indifferent record against West Indies.

Leading the field among batsmen of the period of course is the Australian Don Bradman, and in our current age of computerised statistics and covered pitches most people proclaim him to be the greatest batsman of all time. From a quantitative point of view, Bradman's overall Test career average of 99 is half as high again as the next man; his first-class average of 95 one third higher. Taking just the Test matches against the strongest opponents, which I have done here, he is still 39% clear of contemporaries – perhaps a more significant measure bearing in mind that this was an era of uncommonly high scoring. He also made his runs comfortably faster than all but one of the men of his time. What are the arguments against?

Staying with the "comparison with contemporaries" criterion, Bradman was still not as far ahead as Grace was at his peak. As we have seen, WG's first-class career average was at one stage double that of anyone who had appeared to that time, admittedly before the advent of Test cricket. Bradman did not come across many bad pitches, and when he did, he was certainly not as good a player on them as Hobbs or Trumper. Neither did he face anything like the amount of hostile fast bowling he would have been confronted with today. When he did face it, notably during the Bodyline series, he did not handle it as well as McCabe, nor as imperiously as Viv Richards has done in more recent times.

Although master of every stroke, Bradman was no stylist. Short of stature, his batting was based on early reading of the bowled ball, lightning footwork forward to meet it, or back to watch it, then a rapidly-executed late, but certain, stroke across the ground where there was no fielder. His ability to avoid fielders was uncanny. Like many Australians, most of his runs came on the leg side, from a higher than normal proportion (around sixty per cent) of back-foot strokes. If he had a favourite shot, it was the pull through mid-wicket.

Two factors clinch the argument for this writer: one qualitative, one quantitative. The qualitative factor was psychological. Bradman made bowlers look and feel small, intimidating them to an extent only Grace and Viv Richards have approached, but not equalled. More than one bowler said he felt sure The Don knew where he was going to bowl before the ball left his hand. The quantitative factor was Bradman's consistency, where again he is on his own. During a first-class career of over twenty years, three of which were blank due to war, Bradman's *lowest* average in a Test series was 56. His lowest in a first-class season (taking a minimum of half a dozen games) was 61.

Australia's batting during the 1930s, led by Bradman, was for the first time stronger than England's. Bill Ponsford possessed a similarly insatiable appetite for big scores, once recording 2183 runs in thirteen consecutive first-class innings at an average of 167, but also a weakness against the fastest bowling, ruthlessly exploited by Larwood. His opening partner for state and country, Bill Woodfull, was dubbed "unbowlable", with his minimal backlift and narrower range of strokes, and was more secure against pace, twice carrying his bat through a Test innings. No one has tackled fast bowling more confidently than Stan McCabe, an aggressive yet strictly orthodox player with all the shots. McCabe's scoring rate of 45 runs an hour is miles ahead of anyone of the period, including Bradman, and he still averaged 52 against the best sides. McCabe is recalled chiefly for three of the greatest Test innings, played in three different countries. He was certainly a great batsman, but for some reason has not always been acknowledged as such.

Australia regained The Ashes in England in 1930, when matches here were extended to four days. There remained from 1912 the provision of a timeless final Test should the series be undecided at that stage. Bradman compiled a still-unequalled aggregate of 974 runs, 309 of which came on the first day at Leeds. Grimmett took 29 wickets but they cost him over thirty runs apiece. Then came Bodyline – a tactic devised by some radical thinkers in England and ruthlessly implemented by captain Jardine. It consisted of persistent fast short-pitched bowling on the line of the batsman's body and head, just outside leg stump. As many as six short-legs were sometimes posted, plus another couple of men out for the mistimed hook. The off side was left virtually empty. The main target was Bradman, who had to be curbed, it was reasoned, for England to stand any chance. But all the Australian batsmen were subjected to Bodyline and they did not like it. The general view after the event was that Bodyline was successful but ruined the game. Two thirds of a century later it is easy to conclude that today's batsmen have just as tough a time, but the key was the field placing, which was soon prohibited. Such a concentration of leg-side fielders, supporting an attack of leg-stump bumpers, severely limits the batsman's options and makes for a tedious spectacle. If the bowling is good enough, and it was, then only an outstanding innings can defy it for long. There were three such innings in 1932-33, representing the three possible responses to these tactics. Bold, aggressive hooking were the hallmarks of McCabe's 187 not out in Sydney. At Melbourne, Bradman stepped away further to leg and cross-batted the short-pitchers through the vacant off side, making 103 not out from a total of 191. In Adelaide, Woodfull stood his ground and defended from behind the line, carrying his bat for 73. As far as the tourists were concerned, their objective was achieved, the 4-1 win justifying the means. Larwood's 33 wickets were crucial. O'Reilly, almost unnoticed, took 27 for Australia. Everyone said that Bradman had been tamed, and it is true that his average was "only" 56, but of the batsmen on either side only Hammond and Sutcliffe scored more runs (44 more), and they played in one more match. The political fallout from this series resulted in Jardine and Larwood never facing Australia again.

Returning to England in 1934, the Aussies reclaimed the urn, this time for 19 long years. Bradman and Ponsford put on 388 together at Leeds, and bettered it with 451 at The Oval. O'Reilly and Grimmett shared 53 wickets in the series. England won the first two matches in Australia in 1936-37, only for the hosts to claim the remaining three. The Australian comeback was marshalled inevitably by Bradman, now captain, with scores of 270, 212 and 169, and by O'Reilly with 19 wickets. The 1938 series in England was high-scoring even by the standards of the 1930s. It is recalled now chiefly for Len Hutton's innings of 364 at The Oval, made from an English total of 903 for 7 declared which enabled the home side to level the series. Attention focused on Hutton's passing of Bradman's previous Ashes record score of 334, and there were great celebrations when he did. No one took any notice of the fact that Hammond had made 336 not out against New Zealand six years previously. For many people Test matches between England and Australia were still the only ones which counted. In the first two matches of the series, there were four further double centuries. The most breathtaking was McCabe's 232 at Trent Bridge, scored at a run a minute while eight partners fell in making 68, including extras, between them. The wicket was a lot easier than the time Jessop turned the tide, but McCabe's strokeplay was purer with scarcely a hint of risk, and was accompanied by masterly manipulation of the strike. Fortunately some snippets have been captured on film. Denzil Batchelor saw events in a wider context:

> McCabe had done a unique thing. Many men have won matches off their own bat. On this wicket and with England's sky-scraping score, such a feat was not possible – so McCabe had done more. He had come in at a moment in history when it seemed certain that the sun was about to set on a long period of Australian ascendancy. McCabe, by his own efforts, had stopped the sun, and saved the Australian empire.

Whether it was McCabe's own best innings has often been debated. His 189 not out at Johannesburg was even faster, in a more desperate situation on a dusty wicket, while the 187 not out in Sydney was made against more testing Bodyline bowling. Hammond's 240 in the Lord's Test, his fourth double hundred against Australia, is generally considered his finest knock. Bradman scored hundreds in the first three Tests, but did not bat in the fourth and final match due to injury.

The South Africans had now rolled up their mats and replaced them with easy-paced turf wickets. This hastened the full development of a new generation of batsmen, led by Dudley Nourse and Bruce Mitchell, who could now move forward confidently without fear of being left high and dry by a vicious break. Nourse was an excellent player of slow bowling, and registered the only Test double century ever scored against O'Reilly and Grimmett – a classic. Mitchell was a neat well-organised opener, often slow, who proved a thorn in England's side but made made less impression on the Australians. His most important innings was at Lord's in 1935: 164 not out from a second innings total of 278 for 7 declared, as South Africa won a Test and series in England for the first time. The other four games were drawn as neither side had the bowling to force a result within three days. This was England's third consecutive series defeat to three different opponents: Australia, West Indies in the Caribbean when the best bowlers again stayed at home, and now South Africa.

In the 1920s the South Africans lost one home series to England and drew another. On neither trip did the tourists bring a representative attack. Hammond opened the bowling in all five Tests in 1927-28. Two rubbers in England during the decade confirmed South Africa's real standing, as she lost five matches without winning any.

The Australians paid a rare visit to South Africa on the way back from England in 1921, winning the three-match series one-nil. The teams next met in Australia in 1931-32, a year after South Africa had defeated a fairly representative English touring side 1-0 with a triumph on Johannesburg's mat. That result quickly faded into insignificance as Australia completed a

5-0 whitewash, three matches being won by an innings and another by ten wickets. Bradman batted in four Tests, knocking up 806 runs for four times out. Once again the South Africans were unable to contain an exceptional talent. Secret meetings were hastily convened in London, in preparation for the following winter. Before returning home, South Africa played two Tests in New Zealand and won both. This emphasised the huge gulf across the Tasman Sea, which Australia was not too bothered about bridging.

It is only from 1935 that South Africa can be considered a front-ranking power in Test cricket, having taken the major step of breaking the old duopoly, and my tables include performance against South Africa from this time. However, the South Africans were still a long way from becoming unofficial world champions. This was made crystal clear a few months later when they entertained Australia, minus Bradman, for a five-Test series. Australia again won three matches by an innings, one by nine wickets, and might well have won the other but for a storm in Johannesburg. The drawn match featured both Nourse's and McCabe's famous innings. O'Reilly and Grimmett this time shared 71 wickets. South Africa's final series before the Second World War was at home to England in 1938-39. Neither side had an O'Reilly or a Grimmett, and the bowling completely lacked penetration as batsmen scored more or less as they pleased. England won the only game to be decided.

The number of Test-playing countries doubled within four years as first West Indies, in 1928, then New Zealand and India, entered the fold. None were a match for full-strength English or Australian sides before the Second World War. New Zealand and India did not win a single Test match against anybody until the 1950s. West Indies, as mentioned, did defeat an English touring team by two matches to one in 1935. Five years earlier they shared a home series 1-1 against the same opponents, who had two unrepresentative teams playing Tests in the Caribbean and New Zealand at the same time. It is arguable whether they should have counted as "Tests", and performances against these England teams cannot be taken too seriously. West Indies did manage a genuine Test win against Australia on a Sydney sticky in 1930-31, after heavy defeats in the four previous matches. They were hampered by a quota system which decreed that a certain number of representatives from Barbados, British Guiana, Jamaica and Trinidad had to be included in touring sides. The smaller islands were ignored.

From the new countries emerged two outstanding batsmen – the two in fact who have come closer than anyone to Bradman's first-class career average. George Headley from Jamaica took a great liking to English bowling, twice hitting a hundred in each innings of a Test and twice making double centuries. A sterner examination was that one pre-war series in Australia, when he averaged 37, including two hundreds. No international side has relied so heavily on one batsman as West Indies did on Headley during the 1930s. He made a quarter of their runs – 2% more than the proportion Bradman scored for Australia during the inter-war period. With the scarcity of domestic first-class cricket in the Caribbean, batsmen were unaccustomed to building an innings. An exception had been the fine white Barbadian opener George Challenor, and it was a pity that he had all but reached his fortieth birthday by the time West Indies played their first Test match.

Headley was very much a back foot player, assured on bad wickets, and particularly strong though mid-on. All the descriptions I have seen refer to him as an attacking batsman, but the scoring rate calculated in the previous table suggests otherwise at the highest level. What about in first-class cricket? Gerald Brodribb's work is again revealing. Taking innings of fifty or more in England, Headley scored at 34 runs per hour – the same rate as Sutcliffe and Woodfull, and slower than Hutton.

Vijay Merchant was an even more conscious builder of an innings, founding the Bombay school of watchful defence and exquisite technique which in later generations took in the likes of Vijay Manjrekar, Gavaskar, Vengsarkar and Tendulkar. He was better on a damp pitch than any of them, like Headley being completely at home in conditions which were alien to him. This was well illustrated during the wet English summer of 1946, when he finished second to Hammond in the national averages. On his previous visit ten years earlier, he ended up third. A delicious late cutter, Merchant never had the chance to face Australia. He retired with the formidable first-class career average of 72. Headley's was 69. Lest it be supposed that this was mainly the result of easy runs in domestic cricket, it is worth pointing out that Merchant averaged 62 abroad and Headley 60. Both have higher averages in England than any Englishman.

The next set of averages confirm that this was not a good time to be a bowler. With everything stacked in the batsman's favour, only one man consistently threatened the best players at the highest level, and that was Bill O'Reilly. His wickets came fully four runs cheaper than those of his nearest rival. The first three Englishmen in the list are all famous names, with classical side-on actions which found their way into the MCC Coaching Manual, but their wickets per match ratios are well below those of the Australian leg-spinners, and each made a major impression on only one Ashes series.

Averages of Bowlers who featured mainly between 1920 and 1949

Matches included: *All Tests between England and Australia. All Tests between England/Australia and South Africa from 1935. For players from other countries: performance in all Tests against Australia; all Tests against England in England; all Tests against South Africa from 1935. For South Africans: also performance against English touring team 1930-31. For New Zealanders: also performance in Tests against English teams returning from Australia.*
Average Runs per Wicket (England v Australia Tests) = 36
Qualification: *60 wickets for English, Australian and South African bowlers; 50 wickets for the rest*

	Type	*Average*	*Wickets Per Match*
O'Reilly (Aus)	LBG	23	5.3
Grimmett (Aus)	LBG	27	5.5
Verity (Eng)	SLA	27	3.3
Larwood (Eng)	RF	30	4.2
Tate (Eng)	RMF	30	4.0
Gregory JM (Aus)	RF	33	3.3
Mailey (Aus)	LBG	34	4.7
Wright (Eng)	LBG	39	3.6
Notable non-qualifiers:			
[Cowie (NZ)	RFM	21	5.0]
[McDonald (Aus)	RF	32	4.1]

Key to bowling types: RF = Right arm fast; RFM = Right arm fast-medium; RMF = Right arm medium-fast; LBG = Leg-break and googly; SLA = Slow left arm orthodox

Tate's 38 wickets in 1924-25 was a most praiseworthy performance because there was no support at the other end, apart from the excellent Strudwick standing over the stumps; Larwood's success in 1932-33 owed much to the Bodyline leg-theory tactics and field placings which were outlawed soon afterwards; Verity in 1934 took 14 of his 24 wickets during a single day on a helpful Lord's pitch. Hedley Verity was yet another high-class Yorkshire left-arm spinner, rather quicker through the air than his predecessors. His first-class career average is the lowest anywhere this century. Doug Wright could produce the unplayable ball, as a record seven first-class hat-tricks suggest, but was very inconsistent. This was the time when another leg-spinner, tiny Tich Freeman of Kent, became the most successful bowler ever in county cricket. The best batsmen tended to get after him, however, and he was not selected often against Australia.

Unlike most of the pre-1914 medium-pacers who utilised spin, Maurice Tate's sharp movement came from the modern methods of swing and cut. The new ball went away late in the air; the older one came back. Tate was a natural bowler, in that without thinking too much about what he was doing, he managed to generate as much relative pace off the wicket (or strictly speaking decelerate as little) as anyone. Because they peaked at different times, his partnership with Harold Larwood – one of the fastest and most accurate of pace bowlers, as well as one of the most feared – was not as formidable as those of Barnes and Foster, Gregory and McDonald, or O'Reilly and Grimmett.

After Gregory's retirement the Australians had little fast bowling to write home about during the inter-war period, and relied heavily on wrist-spin. Bill O'Reilly and Clarrie Grimmett were the most successful-ever pairing of spin bowlers in Test cricket. Both delivered with ugly actions – O'Reilly stooped and open-chested, Grimmett a hunched roundarm – and pushed the ball through, giving nothing away. O'Reilly was virtually medium pace. Neither turned the leg-break a great deal, but O'Reilly had a devastating high-bouncing googly and Grimmett a scuttling flipper, along with other acute variations. Grimmett was a key bowler in England in 1930 and 1934 but was not as penetrative against the same opponents in Australia, apart from a startling debut in 1925. In 1928-29 his wickets cost 44 runs apiece; in 1932-33 he was dropped after two unsuccessful matches. And in 1936-37 he was not picked at all despite having taken a remarkable 44 Test wickets in South Africa the previous year. O'Reilly on the other hand never knew an unsuccessful series, capturing over twenty wickets in each of his four encounters with England. Unlike Barnes, O'Reilly's superiority was also evident in other first-class cricket, where a career average of 16 is well below any Australian starting out this century, none of whom got below 20. A comparison with Grimmett is interesting. Away from their homeland, Grimmett's first-class wickets cost 17 apiece; O'Reilly's 15. On Australia's slow inter-war tracks, Grimmett paid 24 runs for every wicket; O'Reilly just 17. Bradman was not alone in proclaiming O'Reilly the greatest bowler of his experience. In my view he was the greatest of all time.

At the outbreak of World War Two, New Zealander Jack Cowie was the most dangerous new ball bowler in the world, and maintained much of his form afterwards. New Zealanders' Test performances against English teams returning from Australia are included in the tables because England had nearly all their leading players with them. Cowie apart, the attacks of the newer countries did not yet pose too much of a threat, although the Indian opening pair, Amar Singh and Mahomed Nissar, were rated quite highly. Nissar came from the one part of the country to breed fast bowlers, and nowadays would represent Pakistan. West Indies relied on their pace men, who were not the force they are now, nor quite of the calibre of Barbadian Clifford Goodman back in the 1890s. One of them, Learie Constantine, was the greatest all-round fieldsman seen before or since.

Test cricket re-started after the war in 1946 following a seven-year gap. Australia as holders of The Ashes remained installed as cricket's leading power, with England still the most likely challengers. The sequence of events between these old enemies bore remarkable similarity to the corresponding period after the previous conflict. In both cases England visited Australia probably too soon and suffered heavy defeat in the Test series, their opponents having all the bowling. The return matches saw England hammered at home, a distinctive feature being the hostile pace confronting them from both ends. During the next trips to Australia, both English teams were rather unlucky to lose by four Tests to one, fielding a medium-pacer (Tate/Bedser) who was the best bowler on either side. The following series in England, 1926 and 1953 respectively, came eight years after the end of the war, and were affected more than their fair share by rain. In each case the first four Tests were drawn; and in each case England won back The Ashes in front of an euphoric crowd at The Oval.

Bradman's team which beat England 3-0 in 1946-47 and 4-0 in 1948, when matches here were lengthened to five days, drew inevitable comparisons with Armstrong's dominating combination a quarter of a century earlier. Both enjoyed a monopoly of quality bowling and fielded superbly. The later side lacked a top-class spinner, but this was less of a handicap in 1948 because of the 55-over new ball rule. Moreover, what spinners there were still had to be watched because of Don Tallon's exceptional wicket-keeping. Both batting line-ups were strong in depth, but not quite as strong as they appeared, faced as they were by such innocuous bowling. This was evident when the sharper attacks of the 1950s made some of the Australian batsmen look more vulnerable. Australia's historic fourth innings 404-3 in under a day to win the Leeds Test of 1948 was a monumental effort on the part of Morris (182) and Bradman (173 not out), but even an average bowling and fielding performance would have prevented it. England were way below average that day. In the final match at The Oval, Lindwall bowled the home side out for 52, a far cry from 1938.

South Africa resurfaced after the war as she had left off, losing two high-scoring series to England and being thumped by Australia. In the now legendary English summer of 1947, Compton and Edrich rattled up 1300 Test runs between them for the home side; Nourse, Mitchell and Melville nearly 1800 for the South Africans. England won 3-0, then 2-0 in South Africa a year and a half later. The Australians won 4-0 in South Africa in 1949-50, gaining a most remarkable victory in the third Test at Durban. South Africa made 311, then bowled Australia out for 75 on turning pitch, Tayfield taking 7 for 23. Judging correctly that the wicket would turn even more as the match went on, the home side did not enforce the follow-on and were dismissed for 99, leaving the Australians an improbable 336 to win in 435 minutes. The Aussies got them, Neil Harvey making a chanceless 151 not out, a truly great innings.

This was Australia's first series after Bradman's retirement. His Test average after the war was actually higher than before: in excess of 100. When he hung up his boots in 1949, bowlers were in need of some relief. They received more than they expected.

6 . BOWLERS' RULE RETURNED (1950-1959)

World's Leading Team 1950-59

Period	Leading Team	Years Reign
1950-52	Australia	3
1953-58	England	6
1959	Australia	1

When batting became too easy, the radical response was Bodyline, which in turn forced administrators to act. In 1935, the lbw law was amended to allow the ball pitching outside off-stump to qualify for a decision, provided it struck the batsman in line and would have gone on to hit the wicket. However, batsmen did not take long to adjust, as illustrated during the 1938 Ashes series and shortly afterwards at Durban. In the last Timeless Test, nine days and 1,981 runs were insufficient to produce a result, before the English symbolically scrambled back to their boat for a journey home where sterner challenges were soon to confront them. After the Second World War, there was the further measure of a new ball after only 55 overs. This affected the poor unfortunates having to face Lindwall and Miller, but no one else. The English summer immediately after the law change, 1947, was one of the highest scoring in history. There was only one thing left which could make cricket a bowler's game again, and that was the preparation of more sporting pitches. This started around 1950 in England. Wickets became green and loose, with lush outfields to keep the ball shiny. At the same time, Australian pitches also began to favour bowlers, who now realised what a gift they had been handed back in 1935. Test cricket became tougher, more scientific and attritional, as carefully prepared field placings caged batsmen in. If the 1920s, 1930s and 1940s were the easiest time to score runs in Test cricket, the 1950s were the most difficult this century.

The one place where pitches continued to favour batsmen was the Caribbean. West Indies played and won two rubbers during the late 1940s:

at home against another unrepresentative English line-up, and away in India, the first series between the newer countries. Everton Weekes recorded five consecutive Test hundreds, and was run out ten runs short of a sixth, but the bowling from both sets of opponents was frankly pretty tame. England's defeat on home soil at the hands of West Indies in 1950 was not quite as stunning as that administered by Hungary's footballers three years later, but the ease of it did make people sit up and take notice. The first Test was won comfortably enough by the home side. Then the West Indians hit back at Lord's, novice spinners Ramadhin and Valentine bowling England out for 151 and 274, and to a defeat by 326 runs. Clyde Walcott, at this stage also keeping wicket, unleashed a string of powerful straight bat strokes in the second innings while making 168 not out. The third Test at Nottingham is remembered for the marvellous stand of 283 between Worrell and Weekes. Worrell went on to score 261, setting up a ten-wicket victory, and then got another hundred at The Oval where West Indies won by an innings despite Len Hutton carrying his bat for 202. Valentine took ten wickets in this last game, and 33 in the four-match series.

All eyes now turned to the West Indians' tour to Australia in 1951-52, which would determine whether a new power could topple the champions. The Aussies had duly seen England off the year before despite Bedser's 30 wickets. The opening Australia-West Indies Test in Brisbane was a low-scoring affair, Weekes's 70 being the highest score of the match. Australia struggled against Ramadhin and Valentine, but got home by three wickets. They won the next match by seven wickets, typically adopting a more positive approach against the West Indian spinners. The tourists were plainly in difficulty against the pace and aggression of Lindwall, Miller and Johnston, but fought back with a six wicket win at Adelaide on a pitch affected early on by rain. They should also have won the fourth Test at Melbourne, another modest-scoring game, after Worrell's first innings hundred. Instead, a lack of experience under pressure allowed the Australian last pair to add 38, to take the match and the series. At the SCG, the home side celebrated with a more comfortable victory, Miller taking five wickets in the first innings and Lindwall following suit in the second. Australian skipper Hassett was the only batsman on either side who could claim to have had a good series. So for the nineteenth year in succession, including a break of seven for war, Australia were champions. They were then surprisingly held 2-2 at home by South Africa in 1952-53, Tayfield claiming thirty wickets and Neil Harvey over eight hundred runs. At Nottingham in 1951 South Africa won their first Test for sixteen years, despite having plenty of batting in the meantime. They lost that rubber 3-1,

Bedser taking another thirty wickets. Australia on the other hand had not lost a rubber since Bodyline, 1932-33. This was their series record since.

Australia Test Series Record June 1934 to May 1953

Opponents	Home Series				Away Series			
	P	W	L	D	P	W	L	D
England	3	3	0	0	3	2	0	1
South Africa	1	0	0	1	2	2	0	0
West Indies	1	1	0	0	-	-	-	-
New Zealand	-	-	-	-	1	1	0	0
India	1	1	0	0	-	-	-	-
Total	**6**	**5**	**0**	**1**	**6**	**5**	**0**	**1**

The Australians were strong in batting during this time, but not that much stronger than England, South Africa or, latterly, West Indies. It is bowlers who usually win Test matches, and before 1950 none of these countries had a bowler with the penetration of O'Reilly and Grimmett, or Lindwall, Miller and Johnston. New Zealand had Jack Cowie, who took six wickets against Australia in the one-off Test of 1946, but his efforts on this occasion were largely in vain since not one of the New Zealand batsmen reached 20 in either innings.

England sent her last really unrepresentative team abroad to India in 1951-52. The forthcoming appointment of a regular professional captain would bring a more hard-headed approach. In Madras the Indians registered their first Test match victory, at the 25th attempt, a few days after George VI died. Mankad took 12 wickets, and 34 in the series, which was drawn 1-1. India had looked a decent side in England in 1946, losing the one Test to be decided, but a more realistic picture emerged in Australia in 1947-48 when her bowling was murdered. Bradman averaged 178 as his side strolled to a 4-0 win. One consolation for the visitors was Vijay Hazare's hundred in each innings at Adelaide.

In the late 1930s India's lively matting surfaces were replaced by docile turf. Batsmen were quick to cash in on the thinner spread of front-line bowling among the many teams now competing, on a geographical basis, in the Ranji Trophy. The Ranji Trophy was encouraged by Gandhi's Nationalist Movement to supersede the tournaments staged between teams based on religious denomination. At the outbreak of the Second World War, first-class cricket in India was 46 years old. In that time, 9 double centuries had been recorded and no treble centuries. During the six seasons of war, 22 double centuries were scored and 3 treble centuries. All the scores over three hundred were made by Merchant and Hazare, as were half the double hundreds. The pair's rivalry whetted both their appetites for long innings. Of these, the most remarkable was Hazare's 309 from a total of 387 all out, against the Hindus for the Rest, which comprised Christians, Jews and Anglo-Indians. In such an environment, the proportion of slow bowlers increased steadily, with significant long term implications for India's Test match strategy.

In October 1952 Test cricket welcomed its seventh participant. Pakistan, formed in 1947 with the Partition of India, fittingly played her first series in India. Pakistan lost her first Test by an innings in Delhi but bounced back to win the second, also by an innings, on a jute pitch at the University Ground, Lucknow. Fazal Mahmood, revelling in the conditions, claimed 12 for 94. India's first series win was secured with a ten-wicket win in Bombay. As the weaker countries began playing each other in the 1950s, their records improved.

1953 was the year Australia lost The Ashes, and her champion's crown, at last. After four drawn games, again The Oval staged the decider. Australia won the toss and made 275. England responded with 306. Hutton, now captain, contributed 82, the top score of the match. Then, as so often on Oval pitches at the time, Lock and Laker found plenty of turn to dismiss the visitors for only 162, England completing a comfortable eight-wicket victory. Their Surrey colleague Bedser took 39 wickets in the five Tests, and remains the only Englishman to claim thirty wickets in an Ashes series in both England and Australia. England's right to consider herself number one was based on the fact that she, and not West Indies, had defeated the champions. This seemed a nonsense a few months later on tour in the Caribbean, when the home side won the first two Tests. However, superb batting by Hutton enabled England to level the series. In the two games the visitors clawed back, the captain made 169 and 205. Ramadhin was the most successful bowler on either side, and the Three Ws scored over 1500 runs between them.

The English summer of 1954 was wet and the hosts underestimated their first-time visitors Pakistan, particularly after an innings win at Trent Bridge when Denis Compton made 278 in 290 minutes. In damp conditions at The Oval, none of the Surrey bowlers were picked. The Pakistanis seized their chance to share the rubber by winning a low-scoring match by 24 runs, Fazal finding enough movement to take 12 for 99. This was only Pakistan's second series. Apart from England and Australia, they were the quickest to adapt to Test cricket, and this was largely because they had a world-class bowler in Fazal from the start.

Still champions, England faced another tough tour the following winter in Australia. The visitors again began badly, opting to field first without a spinner at Brisbane and losing by an innings, left-handers Morris and Harvey making big hundreds. Most of the remaining Test pitches offered uneven bounce, and there is nothing to encourage a fast bowler more. Frank Tyson, in this series at least, was the fastest bowler ever to pull on an England jersey, and proved the decisive factor as the tourists finished 3-1 winners. It could have been different had someone stayed with Neil Harvey in the last innings of the second Test at Sydney, when Australia fell 38 short. Harvey's 92 not out represented half the total. The Australians had lost two successive series to England, but still exercised a stronger psychological hold over West Indies. Scoring remained consistently high in the Caribbean, and Australia's visit in the spring of 1955 was no exception. Walcott and Harvey, in particular, filled their boots, the former twice making a hundred in each innings. The difference was in the bowling, where that of the home side was completely innocuous, allowing Australia to win three Tests comfortably. A closer contest took place in England with the visit of South Africa. This time England went two up, before being pegged level with one match to play. Lock and Laker again did the necessary on their home ground to keep England top dogs. The best cricket of the summer featured Tayfield's battles with May and Compton.

May was easily the most successful batsman when the Australians returned in 1956. His series average of 90 was three times that of any opponent's. The key to England's 2-1 triumph, the only time this century England has won three rubbers in a row against Australia, was of course Jim Laker's off-spin: 46 wickets at a mere 9 runs apiece, including the phenomenal 19 for 90 at Old Trafford. There is a lovely story about Laker's dropping into a pub on the way home after the game, and one of the locals, not recognising him, remarking how it just went to show that the Australians could no longer bat. Laker murmured non-committedly, downed his pint and left. Today he would have been besieged by reporters seeking a rather more substantial quote. How did Laker come to dominate this Ashes series to such an unprecedented degree? It is true, as our friend noted, that the Australian batting was not very distinguished. Harvey, by some way the most accomplished player, suffered a lean time. It was also a wet summer of turning pitches. However, Australia's spinners made no impression at all. Dooland, on duty with Nottinghamshire, was missed even more than in 1953, in a similar way that the Aussies could have done with Frank Tarrant of Middlesex during a sodden 1912. In 1956 their most successful bowler was Keith Miller. Moreover, Tony Lock, the deadliest operator in county cricket at the time, bowled only forty-odd overs fewer than Laker in the Test matches for less than a third the number of wickets. In the prevailing conditions Laker was simply in a class of his own. In their hearts the Australian batsmen ached to attack him while their heads told them to defend. Ian Peebles was one of the more perceptive Test cricketers to turn to writing, and made an interesting observation from 50 years' experience, half of which preceded this series:

> Brought up on pitches of much greater variation the English batsman inclines, in the broadest sense, to be sounder in technique but less prolific in strokeplay. Generally speaking the Australian batsman will attempt to hit his way out of trouble, where his English counterpart prefers to dig in. In a more individual sense it has always struck the writer that, where the Australian batsman always seeks to score from a defensive stroke, the English batsman makes a clear distinction between defence and attack.

On this occasion a little more patience was required. Why couldn't Laker do it again? The following year a law change restricted the number of leg-side fielders to five, only two of whom were allowed behind the popping crease. Laker and others had posted two backward short-legs and a forward short-leg, as well as a deeper man behind square to save runs. From 1957, either this last man had to move in front of square, where less could be intercepted, or one of the vital backward short-legs had to go. Most off-spinners became progressively more defensive, pushing the ball through a flat arc at middle and leg rather than flighting outside off-stump inviting the drive. Tayfield was also affected. Just before the law change he took 37 wickets in a tight drawn rubber with England, making extensive use of two short mid-ons to tempt the batsman to hit against the spin through the off side. It was his last successful series. Laker managed only eleven wickets on the firmer South African surfaces, England's most penetrative bowler being Johnny Wardle with a mixture of left-arm orthodox spin, chinamen and googlies.

Just seven weeks after seeing the back of Laker, Australia's batsmen were up against an equally formidable proposition: Fazal on a jute mat in Karachi. The match began with the slowest ever full day's cricket yielding just 95 runs. Most of the time was taken up by the Australians struggling to reach 80 all out. They managed 187 in the second innings, and went down by nine wickets, Fazal taking 13 for 114. This one-off Test was the first between the two countries, but its real historical significance passed unnoticed. It was the first time Australia had lost a rubber to any country other than England. Pakistan had won her first series the previous year, against New Zealand at home, after hosting a turgid one against India. All five Tests were drawn as bitter political and religious rivalry rendered both sides frightened to lose. The pattern would continue.

In 1956 New Zealand entertained West Indies, losing the first three Tests before registering her first ever win, in her 45th match. The last wicket was a stumping by New Zealand keeper Guillen, who had previously played for West Indies. New Zealand and India were both weak during the 1950s. This was clear to English followers, who saw the Kiwis beaten 4-0 in 1958 and India 5-0 in 1959. The Indians were easily rattled by pace, also going down 3-0 on their own slow pitches to West Indies, spearheaded by the hostile pairing of Hall and Gilchrist. When India and New Zealand met in India in 1955-56, the home side won 2-0. By the end of the decade the Indians had won two series, the New Zealanders none. Pakistan's Islamic fervour, marshalled under the stern captaincy of Kardar, made her a more resilient proposition. On native matting the Pakistanis were difficult to beat. West Indies lost there as well as Australia. But on a true turf wicket their bowling, Fazal included, lost much of its menace. It took a fearful hammering in the Caribbean in 1958-59, especially at the hands of Sobers, as West Indies won that series 3-1. At the very end of the 1950s Pakistan introduced turf pitches, and after a steady learning curve this would be the key to her full development.

South Africa during the 1950s produced the best fielding side the world had seen to that time. The batting was dour, but at last a consistent match-winning bowler had appeared in Tayfield, and Adcock and Heine formed a really aggressive opening attack. The South Africans still seemed to lack a bit of confidence. They tended to play best when behind in a series, rather than make the early running, and the only rubbers they actually won were against New Zealand. It would be a long time, of course, before South Africa would play West Indies. By the end of the decade the West Indians had produced several talented individuals, and had generally imposed themselves on the weaker countries. But their bowling was variable and they were not yet a formidable team. Australia and England were still ahead of the rest of the field.

After easy home wins against West Indies and New Zealand, England set off confidently for Australia in 1958-59, having not lost a rubber anywhere for eight years. In the event, a 4-0 beating marked the end of England's ascendancy – the last time, to date at least, we could be termed a great cricketing power. The series was marred by controversy, notably over the actions of some of the Australian fringe bowlers, but the real difference between the two sides was the bowling of Benaud and Davidson. Both had matured visibly during a triumphant tour of South Africa the year before, and Benaud's astute captaincy was a revelation.

Because the balance between bat and ball changed so significantly during the 1950s, it is instructive to isolate those players whose appearances against the strongest opposition fell mainly within this decade. Qualification for the tables has been extended to include performances against West Indies from 1950, when they established themselves by winning 3-1 in England. Achievement against England abroad is incorporated from the Caribbean tour of 1954, which is when we began to send something like our strongest side regularly to every Test-playing country. As always, all performances against the competitive Australians count. So too those against South Africa, who had become a much tougher nut to crack, not least through their new standards of fielding excellence.

With more matches being played, the run minimum is now 2,500 for English and Australian batsmen, who had most opportunities; 2,000 for the rest. The minimum wicket tallies are respectively 100 and 70. The leading batsmen from the time are all there: Hutton, Compton and May; the two Australian left-handers, Morris and Harvey, along with skipper Hassett; and the Three Ws from the West Indies.

Only batsmen with a good technique could prosper during this period, and none was tighter than Len Hutton's. Hutton's clear lead in the next table owes something to the fact that his career began during high-scoring pre-war days, but he would still have been top purely on post-war performance. 1950-51 in Australia was the first indication that a lower-scoring era was commencing. Hutton averaged 88, with the next highest average on either side being 43. He was captain for the return series in England in 1953, averaging 55 with the next best 39. And in the Caribbean in 1954, he averaged 96, virtually double the next teammate. He is the only Englishman to carry his bat through a completed Test innings twice, achieving the feat against both Australia and West Indies. Hutton felt he never batted better than in 1939, but it was during the early 1950s that his greatness was established.

Averages of Batsmen who featured significantly during the 1950s

Matches included: All Tests between England, Australia and South Africa. Performance in all Tests against Australia and South Africa; all Tests against England in England; all Tests against English touring sides from 1954; all Tests against West Indies from 1950. For New Zealanders: also performance in Tests against English touring team returning from Australia in 1950-51.

Average Runs per Wicket (All Tests between England, Australia, South Africa and West Indies) = 28   x 1.33 = 37

Qualification: 2500 runs for English and Australian batsmen; 2000 runs for the rest

	Average	*Runs per Hour*
Hutton (Eng)	58	25
Walcott (WI)	52	32
Harvey (Aus)	47	33
Compton (Eng)	47	30
Morris (Aus)	46	27
May (Eng)	46	25
McDonald (Aus)	44	24
Weekes (WI)	42	36
Hassett (Aus)	42	22
Worrell (WI)	41	24
Graveney (Eng)	40	30
Umrigar (Ind)	37	27
Miller (Aus)	37	26
Manjrekar (Ind)	35	26
Reid (NZ)	28	31

Denis Compton was contemporary with Hutton, but they did not hit their peak at the same time. Compton's best years were immediately after the war, when his marvellous footwork was unimpaired by the knee injury sustained playing football. At this time Hutton was still adjusting to a wartime accident which had left one arm slightly shorter than the other. In Test cricket Hutton brought all his Yorkshire dourness to the fore, keeping a straight bat, waiting patiently for the bad ball, and playing all slow bowling from the crease. Compton was frequently down the wicket before the ball was out of the bowler's hand, itching to improvise. Nobody played the sweep shot better. Too many others, lacking his timing and judgement of length, tried to imitate with disastrous consequences. Although some of the partners he ran out might disagree, many an Englishman's favourite cricketing memory is of watching Denis Compton bat. Peter May took on from Hutton the heavy responsibility of being England's captain and premier batsman. Though more successful on home pitches, it is fair to say that May mastered bowlers and conditions everywhere, apart from South Africa, where he failed badly in the Tests of 1956-57.

The Three 'Ws', Walcott, Weekes and Worrell, were born within a few miles and a couple of years of each other on the island of Barbados. Along with the young spin bowlers Ramadhin and Valentine, they represented West Indies' progression to a major cricketing power. Walcott is recalled principally for the power of his driving off the back foot; Weekes for his devastating off-side assaults; Worrell as an almost sleepy stylist. Weekes' overall Test average is over a third higher than the figure given here. Only four of his fifteen Test hundreds were made against England and Australia. They were scored at 36 runs per hour, the fastest rate of the period. Walcott also recorded fifteen hundreds, but only four of his came outside the Caribbean. In the two away series where this West Indian side struggled, Australia 1951-52 and England 1957, Walcott and Weekes produced very little. Worrell managed a Test average in the thirties on both these trips, and in adversity was the soundest of the three. Of the main batsmen of the period, he actually comes out as the second slowest scorer, after Lindsay Hassett. Like Headley, Worrell was a more patient builder of an innings than he was made out to be.

When Australia's batsmen were up against it, particularly on bad pitches, Neil Harvey was the man to look out for. Very quick on his feet and always looking to attack, Harvey had the traditional left-hander's weakness outside off stump, but kept playing shots there, the ball frequently disappearing in a flash past cover. Arthur Morris eliminated this weakness from his own game by shuffling across his stumps, but in doing so became vulnerable during the latter half of his career to the swinging ball around leg-stump, a gift to Alec Bedser. Morris was one of three leading Australian openers through the years – Ponsford and Simpson being the others – who were actually at their best against spin bowling. How many more runs might they have scored down the order?

The Indians, still establishing themselves in Test cricket, found fast bowling a psychological barrier growing higher with every uncomfortable experience. Manjrekar handled it better than most of his colleagues but Umrigar was easy prey at first, before he sorted out his technique. Reid was a handy all-rounder for New Zealand, who could keep wicket as well. New Zealand's best batsman from the post-war era was left-hander Martin Donnelly. He did not appear in many Tests, but managed a double century against England. Many of his best innings were played for Oxford University.

There is an interesting mix of listed bowlers. A spinner occupies first place, but all five men to come out more expensive than the average are also slow bowlers. With a perfect pivoting action, Laker was a big spinner of the ball, unsurpassable on the turning pitches in England at the time, where he enjoyed nearly all his success. Tayfield was the better all-round off-break bowler, taking 30 wickets in Australia in 1952-53, 26 in England in 1955 and 37 against England in South Africa in 1956-57. It was sometimes claimed that South African captains protected Tayfield from punishment by keeping him out of the attack. How then did he manage to take so many wickets? He did not turn the ball much, but bowled a very full length from as near to wicket to wicket as it is possible to get, and was master of the late away-drifter which provided that precious movement away from the right-handed batsman. With deceptive flight and pace changes allied to pinpoint accuracy, Tayfield was the most effective finger-spinner ever on good pitches. Ramadhin was basically another off-spinner with a surprise leg-break which also came out of the front of the hand. Difficult to read, he was mastered by the Australians, who used their feet to attack him rather than to kick him away. His gangly partner, slow left-armer Valentine, enjoyed good first series in both England and Australia, and also at home against India, but then faded. The long-accepted theory that spinners improve with age has been conclusively disproved by statistician Robert Brooke.

Ian Johnson was a very slow bowler with a strange surprise ball, undercut with the palm facing upwards. The result was a floater which went straight on like a chopped ping-pong ball. Johnson is one of four off-spinners in the table, the first to feature since Trumble, who retired in 1904. Between the wars it was widely held that off-break bowling was not viable on good wickets against the best batsmen. The revised lbw law in 1935 presented off-spinners with fresh opportunities, which were not fully realised until pitches became looser in the 1950s.

Both leg-spinners, Benaud and Gupte, were accurate for bowlers of their type. Benaud, gained generous bounce from a quickish delivery and conceded only 35 runs per 100 balls in Test cricket, tighter than any wrist-spinner apart from O'Reilly (32). Gupte, at 39 runs per 100 balls, was the most economical of the genuinely slow leg-break bowlers, using the googly for variety where Benaud employed the flipper. Of all leggies, Gupte coped most capably with the easy pitches and short boundaries of the Caribbean, while Benaud has the best record of visitors to the Indian sub-continent. Neither was very effective in England, apart from the Australian captain's dramatic round-the-wicket spell at Old Trafford in 1961.

Averages of Bowlers who featured significantly during the 1950s

Matches included: *All Tests between England, Australia and South Africa. Performance in all Tests against Australia and South Africa; all Tests against England in England; all Tests against English touring sides from 1954; all Tests against West Indies from 1950. For New Zealanders: also performance in Tests against English touring team returning from Australia in 1950-51.*

Average Runs per Wicket (All Tests between England, Australia, South Africa and West Indies) = 28

Qualification: *100 wickets for English and Australian bowlers;*
70 wickets for the rest

	Type	*Average*	*Wickets Per Match*
Laker (Eng)	OB	21	4.5
Davidson (Aus)	LFM	21	4.1
Adcock (SA)	RF	22	3.7
Lindwall (Aus)	RF	23	3.9
Miller (Aus)	RF	23	3.2
Fazal Mahmood (Pak)	RMF	25	5.0
Johnston (Aus)	LFM	25	4.0
Tayfield (SA)	OB	27	4.6
Bedser (Eng)	RMF	27	4.5
Statham (Eng)	RF	27	3.6
Benaud (Aus)	LBG	30	3.4
Valentine (WI)	SLA	32	3.7
Ramadhin (WI)	OB/LB	33	3.5
Johnson (Aus)	OB	33	2.1
Gupte (Ind)	LBG	34	4.0

Key to bowling types: RF = Right arm fast; RMF = Right arm medium-fast; LFM = Left arm fast-medium; LBG = Leg-break and googly; LB = Leg-break; OB = Off-break; SLA = Slow left arm orthodox

The table points to the potency of Australia's post-war fast attack of Lindwall, Miller and Johnston. Left-armer Johnston was the only one who really enjoyed long spells, alone managing four wickets per match. Ray Lindwall had a lovely smooth run-up and action, and as complete control of late swing as any bowler of real pace. A low arm action made his bouncer very difficult to play because it skidded through and batsmen found they could not get underneath it. His roundarm action also caused slip catchers to grass several catches off him which reached them between knee and ankle height. Miller was his country's finest-ever all-rounder, even if it was said with some justification that he rarely extended himself with both bat and ball in the same match. When these three left the scene, the attack was led by Alan Davidson, a wonderfully consistent fast-medium left-armer. Veteran Australian writer Ray Robinson watched a lot of cricket and said:

> With masterly control of late inswing Davidson made top-class batsmen play down the wrong line more often than any other bowler I have seen on Australian turf.

Taking the 1950s as a whole, England's best fast bowler was the ever-reliable Brian Statham, who made effective use of the seam and extracted maximum juice from any green wicket. Of his famous partners, Tyson's impact was brief, while Trueman made more of an impression on the stronger teams during the first half of the following decade.

Moving to the two medium-pacers, Alec – now Sir Alec – Bedser represents better than anyone the change in the nature of Test cricket after 1950. Before then he toiled away manfully, earning plenty of praise but comparatively little reward. When pitches altered, his length became fuller, the inswinger more productive, while those massive hands perfected a quite superb leg-cutter. With ally Godfrey Evans breathing down the batsman's neck from behind the stumps, there has been no more formidable English seamer since Bedser. Fazal Mahmood of Pakistan also bowled inswingers and leg-cutters, with the latter his stock ball, and boasts the highest ratio of wickets per match against the strongest opposition of the period. It is difficult to think of a more devastating bowler than Fazal on matting, apart perhaps from Sydney Barnes.

7 . THE OLD GUARD FALLS AT LAST (1960-1969)

World's Leading Team 1960-69

Period	Leading Team	Years Reign
1960-64	Australia	5
1965-67	West Indies	3
1968-69	South Africa	2

Australia defended her crown by winning in both India and Pakistan, no easy matter. In the eight Tests Benaud and Davidson took 88 wickets between them. The next examination was at home against West Indies in 1960-61, and this turned out to be an exhilarating series. The West Indian batsmen had been encouraged by two more Caribbean run gluts against Pakistan and England, Garfield Sobers amassing more than 1500 runs, including a new record Test innings of 365 not out. In the Pakistan series, Hanif Mohammed played the longest innings in first-class cricket: 16 hours and 10 minutes for 337. West Indies lost the return series in Pakistan, and the home one against England, so arrived in Australia as underdogs. The opening Test in Brisbane produced the first of only two ties at this level. Australia's last three wickets fell in the final scheduled over, the last two to run outs. Each side then enjoyed a comfortable win; the fourth game was drawn; and the hosts secured a narrow two-wicket victory in the last match at Melbourne. If the most thrilling batting came from West Indies, Sobers making two great hundreds and Kanhai one in each innings at Adelaide, Davidson was by some way the best bowler. His 33 wickets came in only four Tests. The Australians' next contest was in England, where they secured another close 2-1 win. The rubber was decided at Old Trafford when Benaud went round the wicket to pitch his leg-breaks into the rough. England were coasting one minute, then suddenly collapsed to lose by 54 runs. Pitches that summer were generally green, assisting the quicker bowlers. Trueman and Statham, who had proved too much for South Africa the previous year, made their mark again, but neither took as many wickets as Davidson. The left-armer also claimed most victims when the sides met again Down Under a year or so later, after which he retired. This was a tedious drawn series with batsmen well on top, Ken Barrington taking particular advantage.

The big two were stagnating, as the winds of change, visible elsewhere in the world, gathered force to blow away their hold on power. First West Indies, after annihilating India, swept England aside in 1963 as they had in 1950, this time with a more balanced attack of Hall, Griffith, Sobers and Gibbs. No Englishman reached three figures in the five Tests, though Trueman was magnificent with 34 wickets. Then a more positive South Africa enjoyed much the better of a drawn series in Australia. Eddie Barlow and Graeme Pollock excelled with the bat, while the latter's elder brother Peter pinged a few round the Australians' ears. What cost the South Africans victory, uncharacteristically, was dropped catches, but in Colin Bland they did introduce the greatest outfielder of all time. Swooping onto the ball in a flash, Bland would often be observed waving the wicket-keeper out of the way. No matter what the angle, a direct hit was always on the cards.

Australia were still world champions, and held on throughout 1964, winning 1-0 in England in a series which enthralled this writer, being the first he followed, but apparently few others. We all remain tied to the images and sensations of our youth. Graham McKenzie bounding in on a black and white screen to be met by Ken Barrington's resolute forward defensive was one of mine. McKenzie was the only bowler to make any impression as batsmen from both sides, led by Barrington and Simpson, steadily piled up the runs. The Aussies then drew a three-match rubber in India and single matches home and away against Pakistan. Bobby Simpson baulked the Pakistanis with a hundred in each innings in Karachi, only for Hanif to return the compliment with 104 and 93 a few weeks later at Melbourne.

The Australians' next trip, in the spring of 1965, was to the Caribbean where they had never lost a Test match. That record went in the first game in Jamaica, thanks to fast bowler Wes Hall's nine wickets. A sluggish Trinidad track produced a draw in the second, then the home side went two up at Georgetown. This time Gibbs took nine wickets with his off-breaks, including six for 29 in the second innings. A drawn fourth Test in Barbados clinched the series. Lawry and Simpson both scored double centuries in Australia's opening stand of 382, but the pitch was too true to force a result. The tourists gained a consolation victory at the end. Conrad Hunte, the most consistent batsman of the series, carried his bat through the second innings in defiance.

Learie Constantine had been saying for years that West Indies would never realise their full potential on the cricket field while a white man held the captaincy. His argument was that a situation which reflected the colonial legacy inhibited the performance of black players. He was right. Only after Worrell took charge in 1960-61 did West Indies begin to look a team, particularly in the field. Now they were world champions for the first time. How long would it last? England 1966 was the next stop, in the middle of World Cup football fever. Our cricketers were unable to match the success of Bobby Moore and his men. West Indies captain Gary Sobers enjoyed a staggering all-round series – 722 runs, twenty wickets and ten catches – as his side carried all before them, until the last Test, by which time they were three up. Lance Gibbs was the most successful bowler, setting the visitors on their way with ten wickets at Old Trafford, as he had three years previously. Sobers and Gibbs were again the stars in a 2-0 win in India the following winter, the former finishing with another three-figure batting average as well as fourteen wickets and seven catches from the three Tests. Gibbs took 18 wickets, as did Chandrasekhar for India.

Sobers was now established not only as the outstanding cricketer of the swinging sixties, but as one of the finest ever to take the field. Christopher Martin-Jenkins summed him up well:

> Blessed with every necessary attribute for greatness as a cricketer, he had rare natural genius, determination, stamina, and a remarkable capacity to continue to produce high-quality performances despite an exceptionally heavy workload, intense pressure from publicity, and the burden of always being the player whom the crowd most wanted to see and the opposition feared most. Tall, supple, athletic and strong, with a buck-toothed smile never far away, he enjoyed his cricket and conveyed this to crowds, team-mates and opponents, and though he played the game with a proper competitiveness and never lost his appetite for runs and wickets until late in his career, he made no enemies. His immortality rests on his all-round success, the style and panache with which he compiled the dazzling figures, and on his unique versatility.

West Indies had now won five consecutive series in five years. The main challenge to them was an indirect one from South Africa. The Springboks, as they were then known, had won in England in 1965, thanks largely to the

Pollock brothers and Bland's fielding, months after losing to the same opponents at home. Because of her government's continuing racial policies, South Africa remained limited to matches against England, Australia and New Zealand, so a play-off with the West Indians was out of the question. It also meant that she could not defeat as many opponents. In 1966-67 the South Africans entertained Australia. Like West Indies two years before, they had never won a single Test at home against Australia, and like the West Indians they now did so straight away. The first match at Johannesburg started badly for the home side when they conceded a first innings lead of 126. Then a brilliant second innings 90 by Graeme Pollock inspired wicket-keeper Denis Lindsay to really go for his shots. Lindsay's 182, including five sixes, was supported well by colleagues, bringing a total over 600 and sweet victory by 233 runs. Australia pulled back at Cape Town, skipper Simpson leading the way with 153 and McKenzie taking eight wickets. Graeme Pollock demonstrated his genius by scoring 209 out of his side's first innings 353, entirely off the back foot due to a hamstring injury. South Africa won two of the remaining three games to clinch the series, Pollock adding a further century and Lindsay two. Left-arm Trevor Goddard took the bowling honours with 26 wickets, showing more inclination than he had in the past to attack off stump – itself an indication of the South Africans' new-found confidence.

By the end of 1968 South Africa were effectively world champions, even though they had played no more Tests. West Indies' winning run had come to an end with a 1-0 home defeat by England, Sobers' famous declaration in Trinidad setting a target of 215 in 165 minutes, to which Boycott and Cowdrey judged their response perfectly. In the last Test at Georgetown the visitors held out with nine wickets down and all men round the bat. John Snow, with 27 wickets, easily outbowled the West Indians. Sobers was again the best batsman on either side, but his captaincy never recovered after Trinidad.

England drew with Australia in 1968 and were due for a crack at the South Africans in 1968-69, but the tour was cancelled after political arguments over the inclusion of Cape coloured Basil d'Oliveira in the touring party. A rapidly declining West Indies were beaten in Australia, where Lawry, Walters and Ian Chappell scored heavily and McKenzie took 30 wickets; then in England where the canny Ray Illingworth had taken over the captaincy. The decade closed with Australia, harried all the way by spinners Prasanna and Bedi, completing a creditable 3-1 win in India and planning to go and knock the South Africans off their perch.

India, Pakistan and New Zealand still lagged some way behind the rest of the field in the 1960s. The first two met in five more sterile matches in

1960-61. It was another 17 years before they came together again, and few complained. Both countries entertained England in 1961-62. Pakistan lost one-nil but India took their rubber by winning the last two Tests, during which slow left-armer Durani bagged 18 wickets. In eight Tests on the sub-continent, Dexter scored 1100 runs and Barrington 800, but by leaving Trueman and Statham at home the English found themselves short of bowling. Indian smiles soon vanished with another 5-0 defeat, this time in the Caribbean, and Pakistan would have suffered the same fate in England but for rain at Nottingham, her bowling cannon fodder. New Zealand won her second and third Test matches when drawing 2-2 in South Africa in 1961-62. This result confirmed South Africa's temporary decline, which had been strongly suggested by the 3-0 defeat in England eighteen months before. Trueman and Statham each claimed over 25 wickets in this series, as did Adcock for South Africa.

New Zealand lost all three home Tests to England in 1963, but held South Africa 0-0 a year later. Each of the five Tests between India and England were also drawn, the visitors again leaving Trueman at home. He had been in a different class from his colleagues against West Indies. New Zealand and Pakistan, now the two weakest countries, drew all three matches early in 1965, adding to the concern over the growing proportion of drawn Tests. The first three games between India and New Zealand were also undecided. In the fourth and final match, India were set 70 to win in an hour, and got them with 13 minutes to spare. Skipper Pataudi and Sardesai were the heroes, both having also made first innings hundreds. Off-spinner Venkataraghaven took 12 wickets. Pakistan then won her first Tests for six years, defeating New Zealand at home 2-0.

The large gap between India, Pakistan and New Zealand, and the rest at this time is apparent from the results of Test series in England. Between 1958 and 1967 England played 24 Tests at home against these three countries, winning 21 and drawing the other three. Not once was there the remotest prospect of England losing. Against New Zealand in 1965, Barrington was dropped for one game for scoring his hundred too slowly – a gross insult to the opposition – then returned to make another in the next match. Taking the hint, Barrington this time added 369 with John Edrich at more than a run a minute, Edrich finishing with 310 not out. Two years later Boycott was dropped for the same reason: scoring 246 not out too slowly against India. In both instances England won the game easily. The implication was that these were not really Tests, but exhibition matches. And in many ways they were. Such disciplinary measures would never have been considered in series against the other three nations, and with good reason. Between 1961 and 1967 England lost five consecutive home rubbers to Australia, West Indies and South Africa.

The reaction to Hanif's nine hour 187 not out at Lord's in 1967 was entirely different. Here was a captain valiantly rescuing his side, and to be fair, he did score over half the first innings total. That avoiding defeat was all the Pakistanis believed they could achieve was apparent when, set 257 in three and a half hours, they crawled to 88 for 3. England won the second Test easily, and appeared to be heading for a comfortable innings victory in the third at The Oval. Coming in at number nine and in the process of playing himself in, Asif Iqbal overheard the Man of the Match already being nominated. Justifiably seething, Asif thrashed a magnificent 146 in 3 hours 20 minutes, adding 190 for the ninth wicket with Intikhab, a partnership record which has only just been broken. It did not save the match, but honour was restored.

India lost all four Tests in Australia in 1967-68, flighty off-spinner Prasanna impressing with 25 wickets, then registered her first away match victories during a 3-1 triumph in New Zealand. Prasanna took 24 wickets this time, and a further 20 during the return series the following year, which ended 1-1. 26 more in the home series against Australia at the end of 1969 extended his tally to 95 in fifteen Tests. His pairing with Bedi (21 wickets) was fascinating to watch, but Mallett (28) and McKenzie (21) were equally successful for the victorious Australians. Australia would not win another Test in India, or Pakistan, until 1998.

New Zealand held West Indies 1-1 at home in 1969, Nurse scoring 558 runs in three matches for the visitors; then lost two games out of three in England where Underwood claimed 24 wickets at 9 apiece. The Kiwis did however record their first-ever series victory – one-nil from three matches in Pakistan. It had taken 40 years. Left-arm spinner Hedley Howarth got 16 wickets. Earlier in the year Pakistan drew all three Tests against England, who were making an alternative trip following the cancellation of their tour to South Africa.

Test pitches in the 1960s remained generally slow, but were less sporting than during the previous decade. Scoring increased, but not always the rate of it, most of the successful batsmen taking their time. Fortunately there were exceptions, notably the two great left-handers Graeme Pollock and Garfield Sobers, and the Guyanese Rohan Kanhai.

Averages of Batsmen who featured mainly during the 1960s

Included: *All Test performances against England, Australia, South Africa and West Indies.*
Average Runs per Wicket (All Tests between England, Australia, South Africa and West Indies) = *34* **x 1.33** = *45*
Qualification: *2500 runs for English and Australian batsmen;*
2000 runs for the rest

	Average	*Runs per Hour*
Pollock RG (SA)	62	36
Barrington (Eng)	56	22
Sobers (WI)	53	28
Lawry (Aus)	48	22
Simpson (Aus)	44	25
Cowdrey (Eng)	44	23
Edrich JH (Eng)	44	20
Hanif Mohammed (Pak)	44	18
Kanhai (WI)	43	26
Butcher (WI)	41	30
Dexter (Eng)	41	27
Saeed Ahmed (Pak)	39	23
Pataudi (Ind)	34	27
Goddard (SA)	33	26
Borde (Ind)	29	23

Graeme Pollock sits very comfortably on top of this batting table, in terms of both average and speed of scoring. A tall man, he stooped at the crease with feet wide apart before simply swinging through the line of the ball. Running between the wickets was not his forte: he preferred to deal in boundaries, natural timing disguising the power in his strokes. Sobers' power was more apparent as he wound himself up before bringing the blade flashing down with a generous follow-through. A forcing stroke through the covers off the back foot was particularly memorable. Both left-handers loved driving on the up. Kanhai was of shorter stature, the most gifted player of Indian extraction to represent West Indies. The shot for which he was best known was the falling hook, where he ended up flat on his back just before the ball crossed the boundary. But the West Indian who scored hundreds fastest against England and Australia at this time, with an idiosyncratic full twirl of the bat, was actually sheet anchor Basil Butcher. The quickest scoring Englishman was Ted Dexter, whose powerful driving transferred itself profitably onto the golf course. Pataudi, a dashing figure somehow symbolic of glorious Indian defeats, managed to keep up the same rate with the use of just one eye. Goddard's batting was more adventurous than his bowling.

Of the batsmen whose game was based primarily on defence, Lawry was most secure against fast bowling, though his reputation was dented late on by two poor series in South Africa. Barrington was the most prolific, especially abroad. At home he was sometimes found out by late movement. Like Surrey colleague Edrich, he was utterly unflappable. Colin Cowdrey and Hanif Mohammed played a good deal of Test cricket during the previous decade, and carried on throughout the 1960s. Both oozed class. Cowdrey was a lovely timer of the ball and another good handler of fast bowling; tiny Hanif very slow with a rock-like defence. I have never seen a better forward defensive stroke. A triple or quadruple flick of the bat between deliveries reinforced an impression of extreme dexterity. Until 1994 Hanif held separately the records for both the highest and longest innings in first-class cricket. Now only the latter remains. Bobby Simpson was less dour than opening partner Lawry; more inclined to use his feet against the spinners. He was also the greatest of all slip fielders.

The bowling averages are significantly higher than for the previous decade, which in part reflects less helpful pitches. Trueman, variable but durable with a dangerous outswinger, is deservedly out in front. The others were formidable on their day, but none demonstrated real consistency at the highest level. Peter Pollock was not quite in the class of his younger brother, looking sometimes rather ordinary on home territory. Griffith wrought havoc in England in 1963, but faded thereafter amid rumblings about the legality of his action. Wes Hall matched any of his distinguished successors for speed and stamina, but not for control or psychological domination. From a run-up rather more economical than Hall's, Graham McKenzie's pleasing side-on action generated dangerous lift from just short of a length, but he was not particularly accurate and went through indifferent series, occasionally losing his place in the Australian team. South Africa's Trevor Goddard was the most economical bowler in Test history (taking a minimum qualification of 100 wickets), conceding just 27 runs per hundred balls. This is four fewer than his nearest rival Hedley Verity. It has to be said that some of his bowling was unashamedly negative: left-arm over fired down the leg-side.

Lance Gibbs' work between 1961 and 1968 places him in near to Tayfield as an off-spinner on all pitches, and he remains the best slow bowler to come out of the Caribbean. Latterly his role became more defensive. Gibbs was the first man to take a hundred Test wickets against both England and Australia. Prasanna, the other off-spinner, was more of an artist, his generous loop luring the batsman forward. Many of the Australians rated him ahead of Gibbs, an opinion not shared in England where Prasanna's achievements were modest. Gary Sobers' bowling was more notable for its versatility, with every possible variety of left-arm delivery, than for consistent penetration. He was most feared with a new ball in English conditions which encouraged that late inswing. Elsewhere, to win a match he needed a turning pitch. The changing balance of power is reflected by the fact that four of the nine bowlers here are West Indian, two South African, only one Australian, and one English.

Averages of Bowlers who featured mainly during the 1960s

Included: All Test performances against England, Australia, South Africa and West Indies.
Average Runs per Wicket (All Tests between England, Australia, South Africa and West Indies) = 34
Qualification: 100 wickets for English and Australian bowlers;
          70 wickets for the rest

	Type	Average	Wickets Per Match
Trueman (Eng)	RF	24	4.4
Pollock PM (SA)	RF	26	3.8
Goddard (SA)	LM	26	3.0
Griffith (WI)	RF	27	3.4
Gibbs (WI)	OB	30	4.0
Hall (WI)	RF	31	3.5
McKenzie (Aus)	RF	33	3.8
Prasanna (Ind)	OB	33	3.5
Sobers (WI)	LFM/SLA/SLC	34	3.0

Key to bowling types: RF = Right arm fast; LFM = Left arm fast-medium; LM = Left arm medium pace; OB = Off-break; SLA = Slow left arm orthodox; SLC = Slow left arm chinaman and googly

8 . THE FIELD EVENS UP (1970-1979)

World's Leading Team 1970-79

Period	Leading Team	Years Reign
1970-74	South Africa	5
1975-76	Australia	2
1977	England	1
1978	West Indies	1
1979	England	1

Any doubts that South Africa was the best team in the world as the 1970s came in were quickly dispelled during her four-Test home series against Australia. The Springboks won all four matches: by margins of 170 runs, an innings and 127 runs, 307 runs and 323 runs. A total annihilation, the like of which Australia had meted out often enough to others, but never received herself. Graeme Pollock predictably hit the highest score, 274 at Durban, but even he was outshone by a newcomer whose effort in tandem was described by *Wisden* as

> a glittering and technically perfect innings of 140, the equal
> of which has rarely been seen.

This was Barry Richards, who made over five hundred runs at an average of 72 in what turned out to be his only Test series. The Australian batsmen were completely overwhelmed by the fast bowling of Mike Procter, in particular, and Peter Pollock. Procter's fierce wrong-footed inswingers claimed 26 wickets at only 13 runs apiece, and he was also a distinctly useful batsman, hitting six successive first-class centuries the following season. South Africa now fancied her chances in England, but the tour never took place as widespread intolerance of apartheid now reached a level which forced the hand of cricket's administrators. There was to be no more Test cricket for South Africa until proper democracy had been introduced. Another 22 years.

Such was the South Africans' superiority at this juncture, with many of their best players still young, that it is appropriate to regard them as the leading country until another team established clear supremacy. This took some time. England recovered The Ashes after thirteen years in 1970-71, thanks to solid batting led by Boycott and Edrich, and Snow's 31 wickets; then promptly lost her first home rubber to India. The Indians won also for the first time in the West Indies, Sunil Gavaskar making 774 runs in four of the five matches against a toothless home attack, but they had been beaten on their own pitches by Australia just over a year before. 1971 was the year Indian cricket came of age, and it was fitting that her spinners played a pivotal role. Prasanna missed two games in the Caribbean with a finger injury, and lost his place to Chandrasekhar in England, but Venkataraghaven and Bedi kept a tight rein throughout both rubbers, if not quite with the penetration Gupte had managed in the West Indies nearly twenty years before. The penetration when it mattered in England was provided by Chandrasekhar at The Oval, his second innings 6 for 38 turning the match and setting up a six-wicket Indian victory. New Zealand and Pakistan both lost to England in 1971, but Pakistan looked a much-improved side, forcing England to follow on at Edgbaston where Zaheer Abbas scored 274, and going down by just 25 runs at Leeds in the one game to yield a result.

1972 was even less conclusive. The year was to open with a South African tour to Australia, but this was cancelled. All that remained were two drawn series. West Indies v New Zealand was a boring high-scoring affair, with not one of the five Tests producing a result. West Indian pitches had slowed down markedly, and New Zealand's Bruce Taylor did very well to take 27 wickets at 17 apiece. England v Australia, in contrast, turned out an exciting low-scoring contest which finished 2-2. Lillee took 31 wickets; Massie sixteen on debut at Lord's, swinging the ball like a boomerang. Snow was again England's best bowler, but it was Underwood who ensured the retention of The Ashes by taking ten wickets for 82 on a sub-standard Headingley surface.

By the end of 1973, Australia had beaten Pakistan in all three Tests, after conceding first innings leads in the last two, and won 2-0 in the Caribbean thanks to fine batting by Ian Chappell and Walters, and Walker's 26 wickets. Gibbs also claimed 26 victims for the home side and seemed to have recovered his form after a lean spell. England lost again to India (Chandrasekhar 35 wickets; Bedi 25), as well as to West Indies, who recorded their first Test wins for four years and twenty matches. Pakistan won her first away rubber, in New Zealand, courtesy of an innings win in Dunedin. Mushtaq and Asif put on 350 in 275 minutes, and Intikhab's leg breaks bagged eleven wickets.

India's bid to become world champions disintegrated the following year during a disastrous tour of England. At Lord's the Indians were dismissed for 42. Australia at long last faced New Zealand again, winning at home and being held to a 1-1 draw across the Tasman Sea. The Kiwis' first win over Australia was completed in Christchurch on 13 March 1974, 18 years to the day after their first victory against West Indies. With both matches being the sixth against the opponents in question, it was a remarkable coincidence. Glenn Turner hit a hundred in each innings, as did both Chappells in the previous game. The only obstacle now in the way of the Aussies was the fact that England still held The Ashes. England had shown considerable resilience when drawing in the Caribbean, where Lawrence Rowe looked as though he might be the next great West Indian batsman. Sadly it was not to be. Dennis Amiss batted for nine and a half hours for an unbeaten 262 at Kingston, and made two further hundreds. The tourists won the last match at Port-of-Spain by 26 runs. Boycott scored 99 and 112, and Greig, normally a medium-pacer, took 13 wickets with off-breaks, despite there being three other spinners in the side. The English also drew at home with Pakistan, and set out for Australia at the end of 1974 reasonably confident.

What England had not bargained for was a fully-recuperated Lillee, whose serious back injury had been thought likely to end his career, let alone an even more fearsome partner in Jeff Thomson. Thomson's slinging action propelled a cricket ball faster than any man in history, except perhaps Frank Tyson. But it was his wildness and steep lift from just short of a length which made him so disconcerting to face. Australia took the series 4-1, then re-affirmed their position as new world champions by beating the same opponents again during the hot English summer of 1975. That summer also staged the first limited-overs cricket World Cup, won by West Indies in a thrilling final against Australia. West Indies had recently won in India after the home side pulled back a two-match lead. Gibbs outbowled the Indian spinners, and Lloyd and Kallicharran batted superbly. But the key man was new fast bowler Andy Roberts with 32 wickets. Viswananth stood up to him best, memorably at Madras when making 97 not out from a total of 190.

The West Indians' tour to Australia in 1975-76 was now billed as the battle for the world championship. Ignoring the fact that one-day cricket is nothing like a Test match, and that West Indies had never even drawn a series in Australia, many expected them to win. In the event they were beaten even more comprehensively than England had been the year before: 5-1. Thomson and Lillee shared 56 wickets, to add to the 58 English scalps collected twelve months previously and the 37 secured in-between. Skipper Clive Lloyd thought long and hard about the way his men had wilted in the face of persistent aggressive short-pitched bowling. The fact that he himself could play it relatively comfortably did not weaken his resolve. If this was the way Test cricket was now to be played, so be it. Soon afterwards, India went to the Caribbean to play four matches. West Indies won the first by an innings in Barbados, then struggled to save the second in Trinidad. The third was planned for Guyana but heavy rain prompted a switch back to Trinidad. Set over 400 to win in the last innings, the Indians cruised to a sensational six-wicket victory, Gavaskar and Viswanath making hundreds. West Indies had fielded three spinners. They would not do so again. Four pace bowlers lined up in Jamaica on a distinctly lively pitch with uneven bounce. As the bumpers rained in, Bedi declared India's first innings closed with six wickets down in protest. In the second innings his batsmen walked in at the fall of the fifth wicket to concede the match. Apparently there was no one left in a fit state to bat. This match made two things clear. One was that the West Indians meant business. The other was that India was now taken seriously, as one of the big boys.

West Indies crushed England in the summer of 1976, Viv Richards scoring 829 runs in four matches, to go with the 500-odd he had taken off the Indians. Roberts and Holding each helped themselves to 28 wickets. Holding's cost only twelve runs each, and his 14-149 on an Oval featherbed was a monumental effort. His lightning pace was comparable to Thomson's, and there were plenty of bouncers. Umpires everywhere were far too slow to act against this growing menace. Except in Pakistan. At the National Stadium in Karachi, two no-nonsense officials Shuja ud-din and Shakoor Rana both warned Imran Khan for bowling too many short-pitched deliveries against New Zealand. When he took no notice they banned him for the rest of the innings. Imran's message was that Pakistan too had entered the big league. This was the match in which Majid Khan hammered a century before lunch on the first day. The only others to have done so are the Australians Trumper, Macartney and Bradman. Pakistan won the three-match series easily amid a run-glut, Javed Miandad entering the stage with over 500 runs. India also beat New Zealand, Bedi and Chandra sharing 39 wickets, as they had earlier in the year in the Caribbean.

The Indians prepared turning pitches for England's visit in 1976-77, but although Bedi, Chandra and Prasanna captured 62 wickets between them, the plan not for the last time backfired. Underwood, with 29 wickets, enjoyed a more profitable overseas tour than usual, and the surfaces also suited seamers Lever and Willis. The visitors won the rubber 3-1, the start of an English revival under Greig, then Brearley, who was on this trip observing keenly. At the same time in Sydney, Pakistan won her first Test in Australia. Asif Iqbal registered his second hundred in the three matches, and Imran Khan six wickets in each innings. The Pakistanis drew this series, then went down narrowly 2-1 in the West Indies. Even with Holding missing there was plenty of hostile fast bowling. Croft and Garner shared 58 wickets in their first series. Imran got 25.

Australia won in New Zealand in early 1977, then beat England at Melbourne in a match to celebrate the centenary of Test cricket. By coincidence the margin of victory was identical to that of the very first game: 45 runs. England made a valiant effort to reach a daunting target of 463, Randall hitting 174 and Lillee claiming eleven wickets. The Aussies were still world champions, but two factors conspired to cut their reign short. The first was a shoulder injury to Thomson at the end of the previous year, sustained when colliding with a fellow-fielder attempting a catch. He was never quite the same bowler again. The second was the intervention of Australian television magnate Kerry Packer to lure away the world's best players for his own commercial ends. A distracted Australia under Greg Chappell lost The Ashes in England in 1977. Boycott returned with two hundreds, after a self-imposed three-year exile, and Willis took 27 wickets. Greig's key involvement in the Packer business did not prevent him from playing – yet – but Brearley was now captain. For the first time it was not really clear at the end of the year who the world champions were. England had been thrashed the previous year by West Indies, who in their turn had been hammered by the Australians. Since then, both England and West Indies had beaten India, and West Indies had also defeated Pakistan after the latter's draw in Australia. West Indies had not beaten their remaining opponents, New Zealand, for 25 years, but had never lost to them either. It was nevertheless difficult to see the West Indians as champions until they had taken their revenge on Australia. On balance one is inclined to award the title to England.

The following year West Indies duly polished off Australia in the Caribbean and took over as leading power. It was something of a hollow victory, for all the leading Australians apart from Thomson had been left behind due to their commitment to Mr Packer, while the home side were at full strength for the first two Tests, both of which they won at a canter. Australia's reserve team did however manage to beat India at home. The

Indians conceded a two-match lead, drew level, then set out on another improbable run-chase. This time the target was a massive 493 and they fell just 47 short. Bedi and Chandra took 59 wickets between them.

At the Basin Reserve Wellington, New Zealand finally beat England, after 48 years, at the 48th attempt. Richard Hadlee took 6-26 as the visitors collapsed to a second innings 64 all out. England levelled the series at Christchurch, Botham weighing in with a ton and eight wickets. He added a further 24 victims when England took full revenge in a three-match rubber soon after.

By the end of 1978, all countries had excluded their Packer players, though Pakistan recalled theirs to ensure victory in the crunch series with India, the first between these deadly rivals for 17 years. Zaheer hit 583 runs in three games and Javed made two hundreds as the Indian spinners looked a spent force. Gavaskar crafted a hundred in each innings at Karachi. India beat a much-weakened West Indies at home in 1978-79, Gavaskar compiling over 700 runs, and then did the same to Australia, her first series win over these opponents. Kapil Dev established himself with 28 wickets, and new spinners Doshi and Yadav shared over fifty. In between, the Indians lost away to England, but not before confirming yet again how dangerous they were chasing big last-innings totals. This time at The Oval they failed by only nine runs to make 438, and still had a couple of wickets in hand. Gavaskar's flawless 221 was one of the most greatest innings ever seen in this country. England now replaced West Indies as champions, having suffered far less from Packer defections. A 5-1 win in Australia under Brearley emphasised this. In a very low scoring series, Rodney Hogg took 41 wickets at only 12 apiece to finish on the losing side, and only David Gower managed an average over forty. Pakistan retained her Packer players in Australia but the home side still managed a 1-1 draw, after sensationally throwing away the first Test in Melbourne. Set a target of 382, they reached 305-3 before Sarfraz produced an amazing spell of seven wickets for one run to dismiss them for 310.

We have seen that it was during the 1970s that the hitherto weaker Test nations began to assert themselves. In 1971 India won series in both West Indies and England for the first time. The following year New Zealand drew all five matches in the Caribbean, and later shared home series against Australia and England. Having disposed of her mats and seen several of her key men take advantage of the opening of county cricket to overseas players, Pakistan improved her away form, drawing in England in 1974 and Australia in 1976-77 and 1979. All Test runs and wickets had now to be earned, and it is appropriate for purposes of comparison for my tables to give averages in all Test cricket. Test matches were increasing in frequency, with England and Australia still playing most often. The qualification for inclusion in the next tables has been raised accordingly.

Averages of Batsmen who featured mainly during the 1970s

Matches included: All Tests.
Average Runs per Wicket = 32   x *1.33 = 42*
Qualification: 4000 runs for English and Australian batsmen;
                3000 runs for the rest

	Average	*Runs per Hour*
Chappell GS (Aus)	53	28
Gavaskar (Ind)	51	22
Walters (Aus)	48	30
Boycott (Eng)	47	20
Lloyd (WI)	46	30
Zaheer Abbas (Pak)	44	29
Kallicharran (WI)	44	27
Redpath (Aus)	43	23
Chappell IM (Aus)	42	27
Fredericks (WI)	42	26
Viswanath (Ind)	41	24
Mushtaq Mohammed (Pak)	39	22
Asif Iqbal (Pak)	38	32
Majid Khan (Pak)	38	26
Knott (Eng)	32	28
Congdon (NZ)	32	21
Notable non-qualifier:		
[Richards BA (SA)	72	38]

Greg Chappell is the finest Australian batsman to emerge since the last war, and is considered by Sir Richard Hadlee to be the most difficult opponent he bowled to. A few critics said he was vulnerable to the fastest bowling, notably Simon Wilde in his book *Letting Rip*. But when Wilde listed batsmen's records against the modern West Indian pace attacks, Chappell was still top of the averages. He faced West Indies in four series, only once averaging under forty. Elder brother Ian was not as polished, but looked more confident against the quicks, hooking them in front of square. Like Lawry, he failed badly on those two tours to South Africa.

Walters is not rated in England, where he could not help himself steering catches into the gully area where two men were usually waiting. There was also a panicky 'periscope' shot when trying to avoid John Snow's bouncer. On a firm pitch against anything but the best bowling, he was a fast and heavy scorer.

Boycott's defensive technique was a model for any young cricketer, but his rate of scoring depended very much upon how many bad balls he received, and even then he did not always put them away. Early on he was strangely vulnerable to left-arm over-the-wicket bowlers.

The best batsman to appear since Bradman retired in 1949 is a toss-up between Barry and Vivian Richards. Barry Richards seems almost to have been forgotten, largely because he was allowed to participate in only four Tests. This hardly made him a lesser player. Between 1970 and 1975 he was indisputably the world's leading batsman, and finished with a high first-class career average of 54. Unlike more cautious openers like Gavaskar, Boycott and Redpath, Richards was a dominator rather than a resister. Complete master of all the shots, and a stylist with oodles of time, he was rather more pleasing to the eye than his namesake. In the author's experience, there has not been a better player to watch. Brian Johnston considered Richards' technique the most perfect he ever saw.

Clive Lloyd was one of the most commanding players of fast bowling, and gave Thomson and Lillee as good as he got in Australia in 1975-76. A year earlier, his ferocious assault on the Indian spinners in Bombay (242 not out) brought a first series win as captain. Before taking over the captaincy of West Indies, Lloyd's Test record was patchy. But on assuming the responsibility, he became the side's most consistent batsman, often adopting the role of sheet anchor. At the beginning of his reign Lloyd was one of three left-handers in the West Indies top five. The others were Roy Fredericks, who was rather more confident against pace than spin, and Alvin Kallicharran, a superb player of the latter.

Sunil Gavaskar is rated higher now than when he was actually playing. It took a little time for people to realise just what he had achieved. A record thirteen Test hundreds against West Indies ought to brook no argument, although closer inspection reveals that four of these came in 1971 when West Indian bowling was at an all-time low, and a further four in 1978-79 when their best bowlers were away with Mr Packer. Like WG Grace, Gavaskar spent hours as a child batting against his mother – but in a restricted compound area in Bombay, rather than an orchard. To avoid hitting other people or damaging their property, he quickly learned to discipline shot-making. The hook and pull never featured prominently in his repetoire. His uncle instilled in him the importance of concentration, of studying bowlers, and of never giving his wicket away, while his father cast an eye over purity of technique, something Sunil always craved. He considers the most valuable piece of coaching he ever received was at a session run by the English professional TS Worthington, when the benefit of staying side-on against the fast bowlers was demonstrated. It must have worked for, though a small man, he was rarely hit. Gavaskar was determined to make India a harder side to beat, and was usually pretty slow. But the bad ball went unerringly for four. With typical modesty he claimed that his brother-in-law Viswanath was a superior player.

> Vishi is better. He has four or five shots for every ball, I have
> just one.

The fastest scorer of this time turns out to be the Pakistani Asif Iqbal. Asif did play some exhilarating innings, notably at The Oval in 1967 and at Adelaide in 1976. No one was swifter between the wickets, or more adept at shepherding the tail. He is one of four Pakistanis in the batting table. Mushtaq had much of elder brother Hanif's wristy application; Majid was a stupendous hooker who never seemed to move his feet; Zaheer scored more heavily than his compatriots overall, especially in county cricket, but was also the least impressive when confronted by hostile pace. The only Asian with a hundred first-class hundreds, but with an average of just 18 in Tests against West Indies.

Alan Knott was one of England's finest wicket-keepers, and the only full-time keeper from any country to appear in one of my batting tables. As a batsman he presented an unorthodox mixture of soundness and impudence, combatting both high pace and spin more confidently than some of his colleagues further up the order. Behind the stumps contemporary Bob Taylor of Derbyshire was at least his equal, as was Pakistan's Wasim Bari.

Dennis Lillee is the clear leader among bowlers who appeared mainly during the 1970s, in terms of both average and wickets per match. A classic high side-on action produced a lifting ball around off-stump, which regularly moved away from the right-handed batsman just enough to give catches to wicket-keeper Marsh or the Chappells in the slips. There was also the one that went the other way, but in general he was not as dangerous to left-handers, and the lack of a good yorker enabled some tail-enders to escape. In Australia and England, Lillee is the most highly-rated fast bowler of the last forty years. Probably the most highly-rated ever. Writer David Frith, with roots in both countries, made the following assessment:

> Lillee had all the stamina of a Tom Richardson, the repetoire of a Ray Lindwall, the speed of a Wes Hall ... In all probability, Lillee was the best fast bowler, all things considered, that the world has ever seen.

Lillee's 167 wickets in Ashes Tests are unapproached, and he also did well in New Zealand. Elsewhere however his record is dire, five matches in Pakistan, Sri Lanka and the Caribbean yielding six wickets at a sky-high average of 90. He never visited India. At the time of the Packer schism in 1977, Lillee had taken 171 Test wickets. When he returned to Test cricket in late 1979, some said he was past his peak, but he managed another 184 wickets at virtually the same average.

The man who started West Indian fast bowlers thinking strategically, rather than spontaneously, was Andy Roberts. Whichever country he toured, his speed and intelligence brought him wickets, but for some reason he was not the same force on his own pitches. England's pace representatives are Snow and Willis. Neither took much interest in county cricket, preferring to save themselves for national duty. Snow, with nasty lift into the ribs, motivated himself mostly against Australia and in the West Indies. Because his temperament was deemed suspect, he was erroneously excluded from tours to these countries in the mid-1970s. Willis, now an underrated laconic commentator, was more effective in England where his leg-cutter complemented inslant from a long run and open-chested action. It was his new-ball combination with Botham, more than anything, which lifted England to unofficial Test cricket champions at the end of the 1970s.

Derek Underwood, nicknamed 'Deadly', was indeed the deadliest spinner on a dodgy wicket. More so even than Laker or Verity. At almost medium pace, there was no time to reach the pitch of the ball to counter his sharp turn and lift. Underwood had similar limitations to other English finger-spinners on good wickets, where lack of flight enabled batsmen to play him as an ordinary seam-upper. In the Caribbean he was completely ineffective. Towards the end of his career he gave the ball a little more air. Bishen Bedi was not as destructive as Underwood on a bad pitch, but more formidable on a true one. The most talented slow left-armer of them all, he was a joy to watch. Untold variation of hovering flight, swerve and spin allowed Bedi, unlike most of his type, to attack on any surface. And attack was all he was interested in. Happy to applaud good shots, but quickly bored by people blocking him out, Bedi took more first-class wickets than anyone in the world during the 1970s, many of them for Northamptonshire. He was not, however, particularly effective in Tests in England. In 1974 the selectors shrewdly pitted left-handed batsmen against him.

Averages of Bowlers who featured mainly during the 1970s

Matches included: All Tests.
Average Runs per Wicket = 32
Qualification: 150 wickets for English and Australian bowlers;
125 wickets for the rest

	Type	Average	Wickets Per Match
Lillee (Aus)	RF	23	5.0
Roberts (WI)	RF	25	4.2
Willis (Eng)	RF	25	3.6
Underwood (Eng)	SLA	25	3.4
Snow (Eng)	RF	26	4.1
Bedi (Ind)	SLA	28	3.9
Thomson (Aus)	RF	28	3.9
Chandrasekhar (Ind)	LBG	29	4.1
Sarfraz Nawaz (Pak)	RFM	32	3.2
Intikhab Alam (Pak)	LBG	35	2.6
Venkataraghaven (Ind)	OB	36	2.7
Notable non-qualifier:			
[Procter (SA)	RF	15	5.8]

Key to bowling types: RF = Right arm fast; RFM = Right arm fast-medium; LBG = Leg-break and googly; OB = Off-break; SLA = Slow left arm orthodox

India is the only country to have adopted regularly the strategy of the three-man spin attack in Test cricket. It has brought its rewards, especially when Bedi, Chandrasekhar, Prasanna and Venkataraghaven were all available, but lack of potent seam back-up has often proved a limitation abroad.

Chandrasekhar has a useful record around the world. Not the most reliable performer, he was on his day the most dangerous of the quartet, and one of the few bowlers Viv Richards admitted troubled him. From a polio-withered right arm, Chandra delivered more brisk bouncing top-spinners and googlies than leg-breaks, so presented just as awkward a proposition to left-handers. Venkat, now a respected umpire, was a more defensive operator. So too, with a similarly low wickets per match ratio, was the Pakistani Intikhab Alam, who carried his country's attack with Sarfraz, until a sharper cutting edge arrived in Imran Khan.

9 . WEST INDIAN DOMINATION, THEN BRINKMANSHIP (1980-1994)

World's Leading Team 1980-94

Period	Leading Team	Years Reign
1980-94	West Indies	15

Late in 1979 the authorities running world cricket gave Kerry Packer more or less what he wanted in the way of television rights, and peace was made. The big names returned, anxious to prove that what had passed for Test cricket during the previous year or two had been diluted unrecognisably by their absence. The 1979-80 southern hemisphere summer marked a significant turning point in the balance of power in world cricket. Australia staged two short series against England and West Indies. The Aussies won all three Tests against England, Lillee and Greg Chappell returning with a vengeance; but lost 2-0 to West Indies – the first time since the beginning of Test cricket 103 years earlier that any country apart from England had won a series in Australia. It was from this point that West Indies' four-man pace attack really got cracking. Roberts, Holding, Garner and Croft took every wicket bar one, while Viv Richards laid into all the Australian bowling. The Australians also lost in Pakistan, caught on a turning pitch by Iqbal Qasim in Karachi. Border made 150 in each innings at Lahore.

With home advantage, India gained revenge on Pakistan, Kapil Dev claiming 32 wickets. Gavaskar made sure of the rubber by batting nearly ten hours for 166 in Madras. Vengsarkar stayed nearly as long in Delhi when India chased 390, by some way the highest total of the match, and finished on 364 for 6. The Indians lost to England in a one-off Golden Jubilee Test, Ian Botham reaching the zenith of his powers with a hundred and thirteen wickets, while Bob Taylor snaffled ten catches behind the stumps. West Indies surprisingly lost 1-0 in New Zealand, going down controversially by one wicket in the first match. Did this make the Kiwis champions? No it didn't. They had been beaten by Pakistan the year before, and by England in 1978, and lost also to Australia later in 1980. West Indies were now manifestly the strongest side. Victory in England during the summer of 1980 embarked them on a fifteen year reign, during which they did not lose a single Test series – a monumental achievement considering the rapidly-increasing frequency of matches. West Indies' record during this time is worth summarising.

West Indies Test Series Record June 1980 to March 1995

Opponents	Home Series				Away Series			
	P	W	L	D	P	W	L	D
England	4	4	0	0	4	3	0	1
Australia	2	2	0	0	4	3	0	1
South Africa	1	1	0	0	-	-	-	-
New Zealand	1	1	0	0	2	1	0	1
India	2	2	0	0	3	1	0	2
Pakistan	2	1	0	1	3	1	0	2
Sri Lanka	-	-	-	-	1	0	0	1
Total	**12**	**11**	**0**	**1**	**17**	**9**	**0**	**8**

The first in this remarkable sequence of 29 series without defeat was decided by a narrow two-wicket win at Nottingham, which was followed by four drawn games. Garner took 26 wickets and Holding 20. Then came another 1-0 victory, in Pakistan, with Viv Richards scoring twice as many runs as any of his teammates. England visited the Caribbean in the spring of 1981, and lost 2-0. This time the leading wicket-taker was Colin Croft, the most aggressive of the West Indian pace men, delivering from very wide of the crease. At Bridgetown Michael Holding bowled his famous first over to Boycott. Six unplayable thunderbolts, the last of which clattered into Boycott's stumps. Typically, Boycott studied the over on film several times, untypically concluding that he could have done nothing about it. In the second innings Holding got him for 1. West Indies' trip to Australia at the end of the year began with a 51-run defeat at Melbourne, Lillee taking 10 wickets. Holding captured 11 in this game, and 24 in the three-match rubber, which the visitors levelled at Adelaide.

The West Indian team now stepped up a further gear to reach its awesome peak. Between February 1983 and April 1986, West Indies won 7 consecutive series, emerging victorious in 23 Test matches and losing just one. 1983 featured two rubbers against India, home and away. West Indies took the home series 2-0, Roberts claiming 24 victims and Marshall 21. In India, Marshall assumed the lead role with 33 wickets, Holding bagging 30. Two fast bowlers taking thirty wickets in India! The visitors triumphed 3-0. Gavaskar's 236 not out at Madras was the highest score against West Indies during this period, but his innings at Delhi was more remarkable in that it was completely out of character. 121 off 128 balls. The first fifty came off only 37 deliveries as the little man thrashed Marshall and Holding to all parts of the ground.

The following year it was the Australians' turn in the Caribbean, and they began by scraping two draws. First, the home side chased a target of 323 in 260 minutes, Greenidge and Haynes reaching 250 by the close without being parted. Next came a narrower escape, with the visitors finishing nine wickets down. Border saved this game single-handedly, occupying the crease for over ten and a half hours while making 98 not out and 100 not out. Then the resistance cracked, and West Indies won the remaining three games. Richardson and Richards added 308 on their home ground in Antigua. Garner took 31 wickets in the series, Marshall 21. The same two bowlers were largely responsible for the 5-0 'blackwash' inflicted on England a few months later. This time they accounted for 29 and 24 victims respectively. At Lord's, West Indies were set 342 in 300 minutes and won by nine wickets, Greenidge 214 not out. Greenidge helped himself to another double century at Manchester where the visitors cruised to an innings victory. The clean sweep was completed by 172 runs at The Oval.

At the end of the year West Indies visited Australia, and won the first three Tests, making it eleven victories in a row against erstwhile lords of the manor Australia and England. The West Indians had turned the tables with a vengeance. The sequence ended with the Australians, eight wickets down, hanging on for a draw in the fourth Test. Viv Richards made 208. Then, on a Sydney turner, the tourists crashed to a shock defeat at the hands of 38 year-old leg-spinner Bob Holland. Marshall took 28 wickets in the series, and another 27 in four games at home against New Zealand in 1985. The Kiwis held out for two matches, like their Antipodean neighbours the year before. Richards, now captain following Lloyd's retirement, made a hundred in the third Test at Bridgetown to set up a ten-wicket win, and the last game was won by the same margin. West Indies had avenged the defeat of five years before, and had beaten the only remaining team to have last beaten them.

In 1986 came another 5-0 blackwash of hapless England, this time in the Caribbean. The visitors were hammered even more mercilessly than before, not one of them registering a first-class hundred on the trip. This was despite the return of players banned for three years for going to South Africa. Richardson made two centuries in the Tests for the home side; Haynes one; and Richards the fastest ever in Test cricket in terms of balls received (56). Marshall and Garner both claimed 27 wickets. This was West Indies' seventh series win on the trot. Marshall had taken over 20 wickets in each, and 181 during the course of the seven. Haynes liked to observe opponents preparing for the slaughter:

> When I watch them practise, they sometimes look as if they
> feel they have no chance of winning, that we are too good for
> them. It's a great feeling.

Richie Benaud, as respected a crictic as any, reckons this West Indian team was the strongest he has ever seen. Sir Donald Bradman considered it the best fielding combination of his long experience, and in this respect it was certainly superior to his Australian side of the late 1940s, which spilled some slip catches. Exaggerating slightly, Bradman once told Lindwall that he would have taken another hundred Test wickets had he been supported by close fielders from a later generation. Moreover, as a main strike trio, Marshall, Garner and Holding would probably have had the edge on Lindwall, Miller and Johnston, and for that matter on any other three bowlers appearing in the same team. The West Indies side peaked at the end of Lloyd's reign, around the Orwellian landmark of 1984. Lloyd himself, an outstanding man-manager, actually rated his 1976 team in England the most formidable he had led.

This was the end of the phase of West Indies beating everyone in sight, but they would still not lose a rubber for another nine years. On several occasions the unbeaten sequence looked about to go, but the West Indians always clawed their way back. A mark of true champions. Where they could no longer dominate opponents, they survived through a combination of brinkmanship and sheer force of will. The first sign of decline came in late 1986 when Abdul Qadir bowled them out for 53, and to a humiliating defeat, in Faisalabad. Stung, the West Indians won the the next match by an innings to draw the series. In 1987 the venue was New Zealand, for three Tests against what was now the second strongest cricketing nation. West Indies won the second match in Auckland, Greenidge knocking up a further double hundred. At Christchurch, the home side needed only 33 in the last innings to square the rubber. Panic set in as five wickets went down in no time at all, but fortunately for the Kiwis Martin Crowe was there to see them home. Crowe's first innings 83 had been top score of the match, and he had made hundreds in both previous games. This was the year he scored over 4,000 first-class runs, the highest aggregate since the 1940s. In 1987 Crowe was the best batsman in the world. The unofficial title of best bowler was a two-horse race throughout the latter half of the 1980s between Malcolm Marshall and Richard Hadlee. Not only were they the most successful Test bowlers around, but in other first-class cricket they always tried their hardest for whoever was paying them, and maintained a level of performance which far outstripped any rival. In this series, Hadlee came out on top, his nine wickets at Christchurch proving crucial.

Garner and Holding now bowed out. As the West Indians sought replacements, two more drawn series ensued, making four in a row. In India in 1987-88, they began with a fine win in Delhi. The surface helped bowlers throughout, turning more as the match went on, and the visitors were set a daunting 274. Richards played probably his finest innings, 109 not out off 102 balls, inspiring his side to a five-wicket victory. India halved the rubber by winning the last match on an underprepared pitch in Madras, debutant leg-spinner Hirwani taking a remarkable eight wickets in each innings. Courtney Walsh captured 26 wickets in the series, striving manfully with his new responsibility. Dilip Vengsarkar averaged over a hundred.

The three-match home rubber against Pakistan gave West Indies their biggest fright for a long time. Pakistan Head of State General Zia was a keen follower of cricket, and sensed that this could be a good chance to take the crown off the West Indians and give his military government a massive boost. Imran Khan had retired from international cricket, but Zia ordered him to dust down his kit and lead the side to the Caribbean. The Pakistanis won the first Test in Guyana by nine wickets, Imran claiming eleven scalps and Javed Miandad making a hundred. In the second, they chased 372 in the last innings and got as far as 341 for 9. Imran got nine wickets this time and Javed another hundred. Richards and wicket-keeper Dujon made centuries for the home side. The Pakistanis had only to draw the last match in Barbados to take the series. They set the home side a last-innings target of 266, and at 180 for 7 and 207 for 8 the tourists seemed to have done it. But West Indies' ninth wicket pair put on 61 to snatch victory. It was desperately close, and remained the only instance during their fifteen-year reign of West Indies failing to win a home series.

The West Indians needed a bit of relaxation and acquired it during the 1988 tour to England. The English did halt the sequence of ten consecutive defeats at the hands of these opponents, by drawing the first Test, but then lost the remaining four – the same number of captains they appointed during a shambolic summer. Marshall took 35 wickets this time; new menace Curtly Ambrose 22. Back in Australia West Indies once again won the first three Tests, before succumbing on another Sydney surface tailor-made for slow bowling. Their one weakness – on pitches offering turn early in the match – was emphasised by the fact that it was the very occasional left-arm spin of Allan Border which destroyed them. No one was more astonished than Border himself by a return of 11 for 96. Only Haynes, with 75 and 143, knuckled down. The next highest score in the second innings was 35. A comfortable 3-0 home win against India followed. Richardson made two hundreds and two nineties, and there were centuries also for Greenidge, Haynes and Richards.

One of the effects of Packer was a rapid deterioration in behaviour in Test cricket. There were instances of bowlers barging an umpire; kicking down stumps; appealing successfully against a batsman who had picked up the ball to return it; running out backing-up non-strikers without warning; and aiming a kick at the batsman. As well of course as all the injuries from short-pitched bowling. The authorities were again slow to do much about it, but in the end they got it right. Limits on bouncers per over; minimum over rates; a neutral panel of umpires; match referees with proper powers.

During the 1980s, England and Australia were not only steamrollered by West Indies, but were caught up by New Zealand, India and Pakistan, a dramatic turnround which was healthy for Test cricket. Before 1980 England had never lost a series to either New Zealand or Pakistan. During the next ten years she was beaten by the two of them, both home and away, as she was also by India. Leaving aside one match against the Sri Lankans, England lost five consecutive home series between 1986 and 1989, to five different opponents.

Australia lost three series in Pakistan, and two within a few months of each other at home and away to New Zealand. In the three-match home series, Hadlee picked up 33 wickets at 12 apiece, including 9-52 in the first innings at Brisbane. He caught the other batsman, the seventh wicket to fall, with a fine running effort others might have been less keen to go for. The Aussies' three rubbers against India were all drawn, two of them at home. In 1985-86, only rain prevented an Indian victory at the MCG, and in Sydney the home side finished six wickets down following on. The return series produced Test cricket's second tie. Australia declared twice in Madras and set India 348 to win. Once more the Indians made a good fist of a last innings target, Gavaskar (90) leading the way, and when the last wicket fell the scores were level.

Until 1980 the New Zealanders had only ever won one Test series. During the following decade they won rubbers against all six opponents at home, losing none, and also beat England, Australia and Sri Lanka away. They were the only side to defeat West Indies, but lost away to everyone at some stage, apart from Sri Lanka. There was less to choose between the cricketing nations of the 1980s, and playing at home tended to be quite an advantage, except when West Indies were visiting. In rubbers on their own pitches, Pakistan beat everyone apart from West Indies, but lost away to everyone apart from West Indies and Sri Lanka. The Pakistanis registered two historic away victories in India and England. India beat all but Australia and West Indies at home, and lost to all but Australia away. She too won in England, for the second time.

Sri Lanka entered Test cricket in early 1982, with a match against England at the P Saravanamuttu Stadium in Colombo, formerly known as the Colombo Oval. Only five runs separated the teams on first innings, and Sri Lanka were 167-3 in their second, before off-spinner John Emburey reduced them to 175 all out. England won by seven wickets. The Sri Lankans were comprehensively defeated in Pakistan, but then held their own in a one-off drawn match in India. The home side finished on 135-7, chasing 175, and Duleep Mendis hit a hundred in each innings for Sri Lanka. Defeats followed against New Zealand and Australia, but in 1984 the Sri Lankan batsmen lit up Lord's. Mendis almost repeated his previous feat, making 111 and 94. Wettimuny and wicket-keeper Amal Silva also made hundreds, and Sri Lanka were more than 400 ahead at the close. The following year in Colombo against India, Sri Lanka registered her first win in her fourteenth Test, quicker than either India or New Zealand. Silva got another ton and medium-pacer Rumesh Ratnayake nine wickets. The other two matches were drawn, so Sri Lanka took the series. A second Test victory was notched up in 1986 during a drawn home rubber with Pakistan. Lack of penetrative bowling, along with internal political unrest, precluded further successes for a while.

Not all was doom and gloom for England in the 1980s. When Englishmen look back for cricketing inspiration, their thoughts still turn to 1981, as once they did to 1953, and before that to 1926. The visitors were again Australia, and it was perhaps the most sensational rubber of all between these old foes. Lillee and Alderman shared 82 wickets for the tourists; Border made over 500 runs, when no one else on either side reached 400. And England won the series 3-1. Anyone forecasting this outcome midway through the third Test at Headingley would have been deemed mad. Australia had won the first game at Nottingham by four wickets, Lillee and Alderman picking off 17 victims, with Border's first innings 63 the highest score of the match. The second Test was drawn, at the end of which an out-of-sorts Botham gave way as captain to Brearley, who was supposed to have retired. At Headingley, England, following on, were still 92 behind with just three wickets remaining. The bookies offered 500-1 against an England victory. Just the sort of odds to inspire Ian Botham. Smashing 149 not out off 148 balls, he ensured that Australia had to bat again, if only to make 130. At 56 for 1 the game seemed to be heading towards its inevitable conclusion, but then Bob Willis psyched himself up, really steamed in, and swept the Australians away, 19 runs short. This was a staggering result. Only once before had a side won a Test match after following on, and that was over eighty years ago. Was it a fluke ? Some said so. Deep down, the hard-nosed Australians knew otherwise. Accustomed of late to bullying the English, they had themselves been bullied out of the game. In the next match at Edgbaston, Australia were set an undemanding 151 to win, which still looked undemanding when Botham took the ball with that determined look in his eye. It should have been a shock when he knocked over the last five wickets for one run to snatch another improbable victory. But somehow it wasn't. On to Old Trafford, where England were just over 200 ahead with half their second innings wickets down. Botham entered the fray and again took the attack by the scruff of the neck: 118 in 102 balls including six sixes. The target grew in excess of 500, and England won by 103 runs. The drawn sixth match was inevitably an anti-climax. Botham took 34 wickets, Willis 29. Both were handled expertly by Brearley, whose calm, intelligent leadership played a full part. Another man with a considerable influence on the result was Greg Chappell. Had he made himself available to tour, Australia's batting would probably not have collapsed on those two crucial occasions, and as captain he would have united the team in a way Kim Hughes was unable to.

Chappell returned against Pakistan, hitting a double hundred at Brisbane, but missed the away series against the same opponents in 1982, when Australia lost all three Tests heavily. Leg-spinner Abdul Qadir took 22 wickets, while Australia's bowling, without Lillee, was completely ineffective. Chappell was back at the helm when England visited that winter, his side reclaiming The Ashes. Lawson took 34 wickets. By the time of the next Ashes series in England in 1985, Chappell, Lillee and Marsh had all retired, and a whole party, including Alderman, had opted to play 'rebel' cricket in South Africa. England's banned players, on the other hand, were just returning. Never have English batsmen made such mincemeat of Australian bowling. Gower, now captain, led the way with 732 runs and silky strokeplay which was a delight to watch. But the stroke everybody remembers is the one Botham played to his first ball from fast bowler

McDermott at Edgbaston. Straight back over the bowler's head for six. A revitalised Botham claimed 31 wickets as England took the series 3-1. McDermott got 30.

When England retained The Ashes under Gatting in 1986-87, some saw it as a fight between the world's two weakest cricketing nations. Each had recently lost at home to New Zealand, Hadlee's bowling deciding both series. At his second home, Nottingham, Hadlee took ten wickets. That summer, England also lost 2-0 to India, and the Headingley Test really demonstrated the home side's deterioration. Gatting took over the captaincy from Gower on a sub-standard pitch ideal for England's seamers. John Lever was recalled especially. There were only two scores of over 50 in the match: 61 and 102 not out, both from India's Dilip Vengsarkar. The Indian seam attack comfortably outbowled their counterparts, and the tourists won by 279 runs. In the previous game at Lord's, Vengsarkar made another hundred to set up a five-wicket win.

A further defeat at Headingley the following summer handed Pakistan their first rubber in England, Imran taking 10-77. Edgbaston staged an exciting game as England chased 124 off 18 overs, and reached 109 for 7. Pakistan made sure of the series at The Oval by posting over 700. Javed Miandad scored 260, and there were hundreds also for Imran and Salim Malik. 1987 was a good year for the Pakistanis as they had earlier taken their first series in India, by winning the final Test on an unpredictable turning pitch at Bangalore by just 16 runs. Gavaskar's masterly second innings 96 was easily the top score of the match, only Vengsarkar of the remaining batsmen reaching 50. But they both finished on the losing side.

In retrospect, the decision to pit England and Pakistan against each other again after a gap of only three months was a mistake. Such was the ill-feeling generated by the tour, which came close to being abandoned after the Gatting/Shakoor Rana confrontation, that England have not played a Test match in Pakistan since. Abdul Qadir bowled superbly, taking 9-56 in the first innings at Lahore where the home side won by an innings, and thirty wickets in the three-match series. The other two games were drawn. When England and Australia met again in England in 1989, people were anticipating an exciting contest between two still-weak teams. Where England had chopped and changed, the Australians had stuck through the hard times with a nucleus of fit and motivated fighters, in the belief that they would come good. And come good they did. Border, Boon, Dean Jones, Steve Waugh and newcomer Mark Taylor all averaged over fifty, Taylor compiling over eight hundred runs. The side's spirit was exemplified by Jones' and Waugh's lightning running between the wickets. Alderman returned to take 41 wickets, the only man to claim forty in a series twice. Australia won the series 4-0.

England, in desperate form, faced their trip to the Caribbean in spring 1990 with some trepidation. Amazingly the visitors won the first Test in Jamaica. The second, scheduled for Guyana, was washed out. England then got themsleves into another winning position in Trinidad, only to be thwarted by a combination of rain and blatant time-wasting on the part of the West Indians, which did much to bring in the minimum daily over rate. The home side then took a grip on the series. In Barbados, Ambrose's eight second innings wickets clinched victory, and at St John's Antigua, Greenidge and Haynes launched an innings win by adding 298 for the first wicket.

Those who like to see bat dominate ball were well satisfied during the scorching English summer of 1990, as batsmen everywhere filled their boots. Graham Gooch averaged over a hundred in first-class cricket, scoring more than a thousand runs in six Tests. Against India at Lord's Gooch made 333 and 123. Not one Indian bowler managed an average under fifty in the three-match rubber. Their batsmen provided rich entertainment, none more than Mohammad Azharuddin whose hundreds at Lord's and Old Trafford were classics. England took the series one-nil.

West Indies faced a genuine threat to their title with three games in Pakistan, and uneven pitches subjected batsmen on both sides to a stern examination. The Pakistanis had their new pace combination of Wasim Akram and Waqar Younis; the West Indians Ambrose and Bishop. With his late inswinging thunderbolts, Waqar had just destroyed New Zealand with 29 wickets in three Tests at ten apiece. Martin Crowe had no hesitation in naming him the best bowler he had ever faced. The following summer Waqar would take a hundred first-class wickets in England at an average fully five runs cheaper than the next man, Allan Donald. Pakistan won the first game against the champions by 8 wickets at their Karachi stronghold, Waqar and Wasim accounting for fifteen victims, of whom only Haynes, with a first innings 117, offered much resistance. Salim Malik also reached three figures. In Faisalabad the home authorities prepared a surface for their spinners, but the ploy failed when its inconsistencies were exploited by the West Indian fast bowlers, who swept their team to victory within three days. Malik's brave seventies in each innings doubled the next highest scores. The last match was drawn, and with it the rubber.

The Australians, having just defeated England 3-0, now fancied their chances, and travelled to the Caribbean in 1991 in bullish mood. Plenty of acrimony ensued, but West Indies were still too strong, going two up before conceding the last match. Marshall took 21 wickets. Richie Richardson was now the West Indians' leading batsman, making two hundreds and a ninety-nine. There was also a final double century for Greenidge and a hundred from Haynes.

Graham Gooch's attritional style of captaincy lacked imagination, but was always at its most effective against West Indies. In 1991 he played one of Test history's great knocks, carrying his bat for 154 on a dodgy second-innings wicket at Headingley to help England share the series 2-2. Ambrose was a real handful with 28 wickets, and Marshall was still there with 20. The following year, political revolution in South Africa allowed that country back into the cricketing fold after a 22 year absence. South Africa had been the strongest side in the world immediately before the break, but had never faced a non-white nation. Resuming her Test career with a one-off match in Barbados, the Proteas, as they were now called, wanted 201 to win, and were coasting at 123 for 2 before something stirred in Walsh and Ambrose. In the blink of an eye it was 148 all out. Ambrose's match figures were eight for 81 off 60.4 overs and he was virtually impossible to get away. The collapse was partly, as captain Wessels pointed out, the result of the South Africans' recent inexperience, but it was also a powerful illustration of the West Indian pace attack moving up a gear when danger threatened.

South Africa's long absence prevented many good players from representing the country. World-class performers like Vintcent van der Bijl and Clive Rice never appeared in a Test match. Neither did Garth le Roux, nor ace wicket-keeper Ray Jennings. Jimmy Cook and Peter Kirsten enjoyed just a brief taste at the very end of their careers. Others qualified, and represented, England: the brothers Greig and Smith; Allan Lamb. In the old days Hick would have played for South Africa. He too chose to qualify for England rather than wait for Zimbabwe to be admitted, and gained a year in the process. Kepler Wessels underwent a mid-career conversion into an Australian international. There were also the Englishmen, Australians, West Indians and Sri Lankans who received bans of varying severity for taking part in unauthorised tours of South Africa.

West Indies' next trip was to Australia in 1992-93. The home side went in front by winning the second Test at Melbourne, Border and Mark Waugh hitting hundreds, and at the dreaded SCG the West Indians were fast losing the initiative when Brian Lara came in and made his great 277.

> An innings of breathtaking quality

in the words of *Wisden*. The fourth match at Adelaide provided the only instance of the closest possible positive result being recorded in Test cricket.

Ambrose's ten wickets set up a West Indian win by just one run. Australia's last pair added 40, and against West Indies sides of old they would have made the remaining two. Walsh ensured they didn't. For the deciding match at Perth, the groundsman prepared a fast bouncy surface, a decision which cost him his job and Australia the rubber. This time Ambrose surpassed all his previous inspired efforts, with a first innings spell of seven wickets for one run. Bishop's pace secured six wickets second time round and the Aussies tumbled to an innings defeat. It was easy to forget that they had come within two runs of winning the series.

Could the Pakistanis now succeed where Australia had failed? They didn't seem to want to. For their tour to the Caribbean in the spring of 1993 they made a quite ridiculous decision to leave out Salim Malik, then the best batsman in the world, and easily the most successful player when the teams had last met. Drug allegations distracted the tourists further, and West Indies comfortably took the series two-nil. Haynes top-scored in five of the six West Indian innings, carrying his bat for a record third time in Trinidad. Inclement Sri Lankan weather ruined the champions' first trip there, then it was time to entertain England again. Any optimism the tourists may have carried with them, from the previous two rubbers between the teams, quickly evaporated as West Indies won the first three matches. England had a chance in the third Test at Port-of-Spain when set 192 to win. They managed 46. Ambrose struck yet again with another awesome display of pace, bounce, accuracy and sheer willpower, to take six wickets for 24 in the innings and eleven in the match. With the last two Tests scheduled at the fortresses of Barbados and Antigua, a third blackwash looked very much on the cards. But England have made a habit during the 1990s of raising their game once the series has gone, and this they did with an impressive win at Bridgetown. Alec Stewart's hundred in each innings was the most rousing English batting since Botham. The last Test belonged to Brian Lara and his new record Test score of 375. The wicket was easy, but the outfield long and slow, and from fairly early on everyone seemed to know he was going to break the record, including the English in the field. Lara made 798 runs in the series at an average of 99. Almost as meritorious considering the bowling he had to face was Atherton's passing of 500 runs. Ambrose finished with 26 wickets, Kenny Benjamin 22.

Later in the year in India, West Indies' unbeaten run really looked about to end. One-nil down in the final match, on a Chandigarh wicket soaked with runs. Jimmy Adams had made 174 not out and 78 not out, but the task was to dismiss the Indians, and it had to be done without Ambrose. With West Indies in a corner, the predictable happened. Walsh and Kenny

Benjamin stormed in to bowl India out for 114, and to take a share of the rubber. On an even more docile Wellington pitch early in 1995, Courtney Walsh produced a fast bowling perfomance to rank with Holding's at The Oval nineteen years earlier, grabbing 13 for 55 to send New Zealand to their largest-ever defeat, by an innings and 322 runs. A leading Indian critic, R Mohan, predicted that the intrinsic quality of West Indian cricket, in particular its fast bowling, would ensure the extension of the fifteen year old unbeaten record for a long time.

Zimbabwe became the ninth Test-playing country in 1992. She began with a promising debut draw against India in Harare (formerly Salisbury), making 456 in the first innings and impressing as a fine fielding side. Zimbabwe also drew her second match, against New Zealand, before conceding the third. The Sri Lankans registered their first win since 1986 by beating New Zealand by nine wickets in Colombo. Martin Crowe considers his 107 on the broken surface his best-ever knock. Sri Lanka had shown improvement when losing by only 16 runs to Australia, after taking a first innings lead of 291, and also when going down by 3 wickets to Pakistan. The following year, the Sri Lankans beat England in Colombo. The visitors had lost all three Tests in India, where Tendulkar, Azharuddin, Kambli and Sidhu all made hundreds, and wrist-spinner Anil Kumble collected 21 wickets. England then lost heavily again at home to Australia, conceding far too many runs. Each of the Australian top six made over 400 runs, including a century, and wicket-keeper Healy also managed a ton. This was the series when wizard leg-spinner Shane Warne really announced himself, with 34 wickets. Merv Hughes supported well with 31. Gooch and Atherton made plenty of runs for England, but the bowling, as so often during the 1990s, was below Test standard. Of English bowlers to emerge during the past twenty years, only one, Angus Fraser, has taken a hundred and fifty Test wickets. Warne has bagged twice that many in the last half dozen years.

Averages of Batsmen who featured mainly between 1980 and 1994, but not from January 1998

Matches included: All Tests.
Average Runs per Wicket = 31   **x 1.33 = 41**
Qualification: 5000 runs

	Average	Runs per Hour
Javed Miandad (Pak)	52	23
Richards IVA (WI)	50	30
Border (Aus)	50	22
Salim Malik (Pak)	45	25
Crowe MD (NZ)	45	22
Gower (Eng)	44	25
Greenidge (WI)	44	25
Richardson (WI)	44	22
Boon (Aus)	43	20
Gooch (Eng)	42	26
Haynes (WI)	42	21
Vengsarkar (Ind)	42	21
Wright (NZ)	37	19
Botham (Eng)	33	34
Kapil Dev (Ind)	31	36

Viv Richards was the most awesome batsman of modern times, and the only one of his generation never to wear a helmet. While most batsmen avoid the gaze of an angry bowler and concentrate their attention on the next ball, Richards stared him out, reasoning that the bowler has to look away first in order to get back to his mark. He actively sought confrontation. Simon Wilde explains why:

> Richards may have given up boxing but he resolved to make himself the undisputed heavyweight champion of cricket. No one was going to intimidate him, no one was going to hurt him, no one was going to stop him. Least of all some burly-looking bloke with a ball in his hand. And if necessary he was prepared to smash him out of the ground to prove it.

Others might hang in there and grind out a hundred. Richards always looked to dominate. Yet he still averaged fifty in Tests, comfortably ahead of everyone of the time, apart from Javed and Border. This table shows how much faster he scored than all but the two all-rounders Kapil Dev and Botham, who were nothing like as consistent. Like Bradman, Richards played his shots late, in a quick flurry of activity. He had no weakness, and there was never a better attacker of fast bowling, despite a moderate domestic record in the Caribbean. Richards' trademark was a walking flick through mid-wicket to a delivery pitching around middle and off stump.

Throughout most of this period, the duty of seeing the West Indian innings underway resided with that most enduring of opening partnerships: Greenidge and Haynes. Greenidge was at his best in England, where he grew up, and also shone in the Caribbean. On Australian pitches he struggled. Like Haynes he displayed an exaggerated technique, especially in defence, with a high backlift and left elbow. Eric Midwinter's 'nurture not nature' cricketing thesis proposes that this has been handed down generations of Barbadian batsmen from George Challenor. Greenidge was a particularly powerful square cutter and hooker.

Desmond Haynes is well known as Greenidge's opening partner, but his best form actually came after his colleague's retirement. The first half of his career was rather inconsistent. Haynes was a model of orthodoxy, if latterly his stance became rather open, and was another excellent hooker. In adversity he was the doughtier of the partners. The only man, as noted, to have carried his bat through three Test innings, and the only one to have been last out in both innings of the same match.

Richie Richardson was initially vulnerable to movement off the seam in England, until tightening up his game in 1991. A dangerous attacking player with a productive slash through the off side, he was quite capable of taking his time over a big score, as a low scoring rate for hundreds indicates. So too was Martin Crowe, a really classy bat, the best to come out of New Zealand.

Javed Miandad has been Pakistan's finest batsman. A heavier scorer than Hanif and less defensive. There were mutterings that the discrepancy between his home and away record owed something to a virtual immunity from lbw decisions from the umpires of his native land, but his average in Tests outside Pakistan was 45, so there can be no argument about his quality. Miandad boasts an average in the mid-sixties for home Tests, and there other ways to be out than lbw. During his early career he tended to shuffle across the crease and get too square-on, but among contemporaries only Desmond Haynes was as adept at keeping the lifting ball down.

Allan Border was very much a left-handed left-hander, in that his bottom hand led prominently. He was not therefore a stylist like Gower. In fact

Border was not a particularly attractive player to watch, but he proved a very resilient, consistent and competent one, against both pace and spin, and scored more runs in Test cricket than anyone. The only bowler who really troubled him was Curtly Ambrose.

It is interesting to see that Gooch scored his hundreds faster than Gower, but recorded a lower Test average. The dashing roundhead versus the more consistent cavalier! English batsmen have not fared too well when confronted by fast bowling in recent times, but Gooch was an admirable exception, playing two superb innings at Headingley against West Indies and Pakistan. He was not as confident with the fast-medium swingers, against whom he tended to play across the front pad.

A glance at the next table reveals the hold exerted by fast bowlers since 1980. Only one of the ten names is a spinner and he is at the bottom of the pile. Comparing these pace men is a difficult business, and opinions not surprisingly differ. It is fair to say that each of the first five – those with averages of 23 or less – was top-bracket. A large gap of five runs per wicket separates them from the rest. Holding was the fastest, but did not gain much lateral movement from a beautifully smooth approach and action. His fourteen wickets at The Oval in 1976, when the pitch offered absolutely nothing, remains arguably the finest performance by a quick bowler in a Test match.

Hadlee modelled himself on Lillee, down to the flat-footed approach, and captured the same high five wickets per match. The raw pace of his early days was reined in off a shortened run, sharp swing and seam movement being tightly controlled from an action Mike Selvey likened to cream being poured from a jug. Meticulous planning was an integral part of the operation. Hadlee's length was fuller than most, but he terrorised the Australians more than any West Indian. At one point they resorted to announcing publically that he had not really psyched them out – an extraordinary move. On a flat track he was not as formidable as the leading West Indians, Marshall outbowling him in the showpiece MCC Bicentenary Match at Lord's in 1987. Hadlee's importance to New Zealand in Test cricket can be gauged by the fact that the nearest countryman to his 431 wickets is Morrison with 160. It is no exaggeration to say that when he retired, that country ceased to be a major cricketing power. Graham Gooch once said that batting against the Kiwis was like facing a World Eleven at one end and Ilford Seconds at the other.

Averages of Bowlers who featured mainly between 1980 and 1994, but not from January 1998

Matches included: All Tests.
Average Runs per Wicket = 31
Qualification: 200 wickets

	Type	Average	Wickets Per Match
Marshall (WI)	RF	20	4.6
Garner (WI)	RF	20	4.4
Hadlee (NZ)	RFM	22	5.0
Imran Khan (Pak)	RF	22	4.1
Holding (WI)	RF	23	4.1
Hughes MG (Aus)	RF	28	4.0
McDermott (Aus)	RF	28	4.0
Botham (Eng)	RFM	28	3.7
Kapil Dev (Ind)	RFM	29	3.3
Abdul Qadir (Pak)	LBG	32	3.5

Key to bowling types: RF = Right arm fast; RFM = Right arm fast-medium; LBG = Leg-break and googly

On all pitches it is probable that the right man is at the top of the table. With a sprint to the wicket and quick open-chested arm action, Malcolm Marshall was a skidder, like Larwood feared more than bigger men. He hit a lot of batsmen, and when pitching up swung either way. Marshall took over 30 wickets in a series in both India and England, 28 in Australia and 27 twice in the Caribbean. 6 feet 8 inches Joel Garner was sometimes considered a stock bowler, yet took more wickets per match than either Roberts or Holding, who often took the new ball ahead of him. When Garner himself was given the new ball in 1984, he bent his back to produce some of the most devastating bowling any batsman has had to face. Garner generated exceptional bounce, but also swung the ball and was extremely accurate. Of all bowlers, his length was the most difficult to pick, and no one has produced a better yorker. He was certainly the greatest one-day bowler, boasting the lowest average and economy rate, and among the best also in Test cricket, where he has been somewhat underrated.

At the turn of the 1980s, Ian Botham was an excellent fast-medium bowler with a marvellous outswinger. Like Trueman before, his own evident self-belief gave England an invaluable psychological boost. Sadly it was not long before his bowling declined, though he did raise himself to take 34 wickets against the Australians in 1981, and 31 when they came again in 1985. Although Botham is England's leading wicket-taker in Tests, he is recalled chiefly for his batting. The mark of a true all-rounder. Kapil Dev's batting and bowling averages are similar to Botham's, and he was an even faster scorer, once striking four sixes off consecutive balls to save a follow-on. Three of Kapil's eight Test hundreds came against West Indies, whereas his English rival never reached three figures against these opponents. Kapil Dev's bowling was also fast-medium in pace, making good use of the outswinger, and was more successful in Australia and West Indies than in England. So used to slow pitches, his eyes lit up when he saw a bouncy one. Taking their careers as a whole, neither Kapil Dev nor Botham was in the same class as a bowler as the Pakistani all-rounder Imran Khan. Imran's most potent weapon was his ability to swing the ball either way at pace. With the old ball he was the first to realise the full potential of reverse swing, though it was not known as such at the time. Unlike the vast majority of purveyors of fast bowling, he was not afraid as a batsman to stand up to it himself, and merrily traded bouncers with the West Indians. Probably his most satisfying triumph was leading Pakistan to their only series win in India in 1986-87. Four years earlier he took a remarkable 40 wickets against the same opponents on the stodgy pitches of his homeland.

Craig McDermott is the only Australian to take 30 wickets in an Ashes series in both England and Australia. Bedser remains the only bowler to do so for England. McDermott and fellow countryman Hughes have identical figures in my table. The latter's appearance and antics were reminiscent of a silent-movie villain.

The difference between Abdul Qadir's home and away records in Test cricket is remarkable. With Allah's sun on his back, he took 168 wickets at an average of 26; outside Pakistan 68 wickets at a very expensive 47 runs apiece. On his own patch, Qadir's variety and disguise brought forth all manner of superlatives. Carl Hooper rated him ahead of Warne. John Emburey said he was the best slow bowler he ever saw. But his failure to adapt abroad prevents one from placing him up with the leading leg-spinners.

10 . THE CURRENT SCENE (1995-1998)

World's Leading Team 1995-1997

Period	Leading Team	Years Reign
1995-97	Australia	3

In the spring of 1995, Australia set off for the Caribbean under Mark Taylor to attempt yet again to dislodge the West Indians. Taylor stands head and shoulders above Test captains of the 1990s, and his side had a focus and determination about it, without the over-aggression of some of its predecessors. West Indies, champions for so long, looked a trifle complacent. They took first knock in the first Test at Bridgetown, and were dismissed for an inadequate 196, Lara contributing 65 before walking for a bump ball. The Australians worked their way steadily to 346, the skipper grafting 55, before Steve Waugh (65) and wicket-keeper Healy (74 not out) played some shots. The home side's second innings performance was even more lackadaisical than their first – 189 all out – and the few required runs were knocked off without loss. The second match in Antigua was ruined by the weather, then a dreadful Port-of-Spain surface allowed West Indies back with a nine-wicket win, Ambrose returning match figures of 9 for 65. In the fourth and final Test in Jamaica, West Indies skipper Richie Richardson made a good hundred going in first, but received scant support as his side were out for 265. The Waugh twins then really showed what they were made of, putting together a partnership of 231 in the face of some frighteningly hostile bowling. Steve's 200 was the most important of several key knocks he has played for his country. It demoralised the West Indians, who lost the match by an innings, to concede a series for the first time since 1980, and a home series for the first time since 1973.

Everyone proclaimed the Australians champions, but it was not quite as simple as that. A few months before they had lost in Pakistan, alleging attempted bribery, and had not beaten South Africa in a rubber since 1958.

111

The South Africans had been world champions prior to their expulsion, but had lost that one-off match to West Indies on their return in 1992. They had since beaten India, Pakistan, New Zealand and Sri Lanka, and had been held to a draw in England when Malcolm blasted them out at The Oval. Two series against Australia had also both been drawn. In Sydney the Australians made their now familiar hash of chasing a small last-innings total, failing by six runs to reach 117. All things considered, Australia had to beat Pakistan in a three-match home rubber at the end of the year to take the crown. They won the opener at the Gabba by an innings, Steve Waugh (112 not out) carrying on his fine form and Shane Warne taking 11 for 77. The second match in Hobart, Tasmania, saw the series and the unofficial title sewn up, thanks largely to Taylor's 123 and McGrath's eight wickets. Pakistan gained a consolation win at the SCG, leg-spinner Mushtaq Ahmed claiming nine wickets for the second match in succession.

A year later it was difficult to decide who was cricket's leading power. Australia lost a one-off Test in New Delhi by seven wickets when the Indians, encouraged by Warne's absence, prepared a pitch which turned throughout. Wrist-spinner Kumble took nine wickets as the visitors were dismissed for 182 and 234. Keeper Mongia grafted a patient 152. By the end of 1996, India had also beaten South Africa at home, by two matches to one. The Indians were one match down in the return series as the new year came in, but with two games to go the rubber had yet to be decided. India had not lost a home series since Pakistan beat her in 1986-87, but had never avenged that defeat, nor the one suffered in the Caribbean in 1989. More recently, the Indians had gone down in England in 1996. Taking the last series against each opponent, which was either won or lost, the only team with just one loss against its name was West Indies, who had beaten everyone apart from Australia. Their one completed contest in 1996 was a comfortable home win over New Zealand. However, West Indies' last rubbers against three countries, England, India and Sri Lanka, had been drawn, whereas Australia had beaten five of her opponents. On balance, Australia's victory over West Indies the year before tips the scales in her favour. As 1997 came in, the two countries were actually in the middle of a five-match series in Australia. The hosts won the first two Tests, Healy scoring 161 not out at Brisbane, then made three changes, two of them unnecessary, for the next game at Melbourne. Sensing uncertainty in the enemy ranks, Ambrose grabbed 9 for 72 in the match as West Indies won by six wickets. But Australia settled matters early in the new year with an innings victory in Adelaide. Michael Bevan, supposedly chosen for his batting, picked up ten wickets with chinamen and googlies. As usual, the visitors won in Perth, Lara (132) finding his form rather too late. Throughout the tour he was troubled by Glenn McGrath's round the wicket angle and movement towards the slips. McGrath ended up with 26 wickets.

Soon afterwards, the Australians at long last took their revenge on South Africa. They won the first Test by an innings in Johannesburg, Steve Waugh and Blewett adding 385, and the second at Port Elizabeth by a nailbiting two wickets. Set 270, the highest score of the match, Australia were guided home by Mark Waugh's 116, which he considers his best century at any level. Once more they eased up with the rubber decided, and allowed the home team a consolation win. Australia now had the better of everyone, in most recent series, apart from India. In 1997, the Indians suffered defeat in both South Africa and West Indies. The West Indians fell badly away in Pakistan, losing all three matches heavily. Australia's two other series during the year were a 3-2 win in England, where McGrath took 36 wickets, Warne 24, and Steve Waugh scored a hundred in each innings at Old Trafford. And a 2-0 home victory over New Zealand, when Warne claimed a further 19 wickets.

Zimbabwe tasted victory in her eleventh Test, three sooner than Sri Lanka. It was in Harare and the opponents were Pakistan. Grant Flower put on 269 with brother Andy, then a further 233 with Whittall. Opening bowler Heath Streak took nine wickets; and the margin was a handsome innings and 64. The Pakistanis came back in the other two games to take the series. Zimbabwe's first Test against England produced a unique result: a draw with the scores level. England had four wickets in hand.

The brilliance of Sri Lanka's World Cup victory in 1996 brought the prowess of her batsmen to the public eye. The following year in Colombo they compiled the highest ever Test total, 952 for 6, eclipsing England's effort at The Oval in 1938. Jayasuriya made 340, sharing a new Test record partnership of 576 with Mahanama (225). Aravinda de Silva contributed 126. This came in reply to an Indian total of 537 for 8, in which Sidhu, Tendulkar and Azharuddin also made hundreds. There was no time for any second innings. The follow-up match was another high-scoring draw. Jayasuriya got 199 this time, de Silva a hundred in each innings, while Tendulkar, Azharuddin and Ganguly all reached three figures for India.

Batting first in a Test match was for a long time a keenly sought-after advantage, virtually never spurned. Until the four-man West Indian pace attacks came along. A further factor now is the increasing number of pitches which, assisted by total covering, seem to play more easily as the match goes on. Only eleven times in history has the team batting last made the highest score of the match to win. Seven of those instances have come in the last fifteen years; three in 1998 alone. In January in Colombo, Sri Lanka made 326-5 against Zimbabwe, Aravinda de Silva 143 not out. Then, within little over a week of each other, came the two Trinidad epics between West Indies and England. They were staged at the same venue after the unprecedented abandonment at Sabina Park, after less than an hour's play, because the relaid pitch was deemed too dangerous. In the first Trinidad game, West Indies, set 282, looked beaten at 124-5, but Carl Hooper (94 not out) played his most responsible innings to bring a three wicket victory. England were crestfallen, and few expected them so soon afterwards to make the 225 required in another low-scoring contest. Atherton and Stewart put on 129 for the first wicket. Then a collapse, and frequent rain interruptions, kept everyone on the edge of their seats. Eventually England's resolve got them home, by an identical margin to that by which they had lost the previous match. West Indies took the series 3-1, Ambrose claiming 30 wickets at 14 apiece, and Fraser 27 for the tourists.

Champions Australia saw off another challenge from South Africa, courtesy of an innings win in Sydney. Warne bagged 11 wickets on his favourite ground and Mark Waugh made a hundred. The Aussies only survived in Adelaide through uncharacteristic dropped catches by their opponents, finishing seven wickets down. Mark Waugh, the chief benefactor, was still there at the end with 115. Taylor carried his bat through the first innings for 169. Since returning to the Test arena, South Africa's batting has made up partly in depth what it has lacked in quality, especially since Wessels' retirement, and no one has demonstrated this better than Pat Symcox. There were those who wondered why the burly thirty-something off-spinner was in the side. Surely there were better slow bowlers in the country. Contortionist Paul Adams for one. True, Symcox took a vital 3-8 when South Africa shot out Pakistan for 92 at Faisalabad, winning the match by 53 runs and the series one-nil. He also made 81 at number nine in this game and, when promoted in the second innings, top-scored with 55. In the Adelaide Test just mentioned, Symcox was put in number eleven, and slammed 54 off 42 balls. But his greatest triumph took place at The Wanderers in the return series against Pakistan, a good contest between two well-matched sides. Entering one place higher this time at number ten, Symcox laid into Waqar and company to complete a stunning 108 off 157 deliveries. He was then dropped for the rest of the series.

Australia failed yet again in India, going down in the first two Tests before winning their first match there since Bill Lawry was captain. Much was made of the personal battle between Tendulkar and Warne, and there was no doubt who won it. The young Indian warmed up with a pre-Test double century off the tourists, then added a couple of big hundreds in the games that mattered. Getting down the wicket decisively and often, he dispatched Warne to every corner of various grounds, dominating the leg-spinner to a degree that no one else has attempted, let alone achieved. Australia remain champions only because they are still able to beat everybody else. In March 1998, for the first time four Test matches took place on the same day, only New Zealand not playing.

The last of these tables cover leading current players who have appeared in Test cricket between 1 January and 31 August 1998, the end of the English international season. The qualification is a lower 4,000 runs for batsmen and 150 wickets for bowlers, to allow for the fact that their careers are still running.

Averages of Current Batsmen who appeared between January and August 1998

Matches included: All Tests.
Average Runs per Wicket in the 1990s (1/90 to 8/98) = 30   *x 1.33 = 40*
Qualification: 4000 runs

	Average	*Runs per Hour*
Tendulkar (Ind)	54	28
Lara (WI)	51	33
Waugh SR (Aus)	48	24
Azharuddin (Ind)	45	27
Waugh ME (Aus)	43	25
de Silva PA (SL)	43	23
Taylor (Aus)	42	20
Stewart (Eng)	41	22
Atherton (Eng)	39	18
Ranatunga A (SL)	35	24

Brian Lara is one of the three greatest left-handed batsmen, along with Sobers and Pollock. Whenever he arrives at the crease there is a change in tempo, with the fielding side thrown suddenly on the defensive. Shorter of stature than the other two, Lara's dancing feet make room for him to play devastatingly through the off-side, and his leg-glancing is exceptionally fine. A very high backlift announces supreme confidence, without quite the arrogance of Viv Richards. There was an air of inevitability about his beating both Test and first-class highest scores. He went out with the specific intention of setting new records, and did so. Inevitably his failures are exaggerated, as a Test average of 51 indicates. At 33 runs per hour, Lara's scoring rate is comfortably faster than any current leading player.

Sachin Tendulkar demonstrates the superb technique of his illustrious predecessors from the Bombay school. More adventurous than Merchant or Gavaskar, he is not quite as secure, which is why he bats at number four rather than opening. Tendulkar has played brilliant Test innings in every country he has visited, as well as throughout his native land, and is without question a great batsman. Mohammad Azharuddin is scintillatingly wristy and exceptionally strong through the leg side, but also vulnerable to the extra bounce in Australia, South Africa and the Caribbean where he did not bother to modify his technique. One would not back him under pressure there against the quicks.

Steve Waugh is gritty and reliable, the Australian most opponents like to see the back of. It was a mistake of Mike Atherton's to state publically that Waugh did not relish the short-pitched ball, because it made him doubly determined not to lose his wicket to it, no matter how many times he gets hit. Steve likes to go back in defence and has a somewhat jerky style, unlike twin brother Mark, who is all relaxed ease, from his stance onwards. Mark Waugh is more of a gambler, less consistent, and the finest all-round fielder in the game today. So confident is he of his reflexes that he actually watches the bowler from silly mid-off! Left-hander Mark Taylor enjoyed a wonderfully prolific start to his Test career, but latterly something went wrong with his footwork. He is an excellent first slip to the fast bowlers, if not quite as quick as Mark Waugh to react to the spinners. Taylor is one of Australia's best half-dozen captains.

The Sri Lankan Aravinda de Silva is a gifted strokemaker who has scored a lot of runs during the past year or so. Before that he returned rather too many low scores for someone of his class. Ranatunga played in Sri Lanka's first Test back in 1982, and his experience as captain has been important. Mike Atherton and Alec Stewart have been England's most accomplished batsmen taking the decade as a whole. From his Cambridge days, Atherton has been accustomed to fighting losing battles, and bases his game very much on defence. 18 runs an hour is slow. Extremely tough and tenacious, he has taken a lot out of himself in his country's cause. Alec Stewart' scoring rate for centuries is not as high as one might expect. A nice timer of the ball who likes to carry the attack to the fast bowlers, Stewart is also an adequate wicket-keeper. The dilemma for the selectors has been that when he does keep, he tends to make less runs.

Averages of Current Bowlers who appeared between January and August 1998

Matches included: All Tests.
Average Runs per Wicket in the 1990s (1/90 to 8/98) = 30
Qualificaton: 150 wickets

	Type	*Average*	*Wickets Per Match*
Waqar Younis (Pak)	RF	21	5.0
Ambrose (WI)	RF	21	4.2
Donald (SA)	RF	22	5.0
Wasim Akram (Pak)	LF	22	4.3
McGrath (Aus)	RF	23	4.4
Warne (Aus)	LBG	24	4.6
Bishop (WI)	RF	24	3.7
Walsh (WI)	RF	25	3.6
Muralitharan (SL)	OB	26	4.8
Fraser (Eng)	RMF	26	3.9
Mushtaq Ahmed (Pak)	LBG	27	4.2
Kumble (Ind)	LBG	28	4.2

Key to bowling types: RF = Right arm fast; RMF = Right arm medium-fast; LF = Left arm fast; LBG = Leg-break and googly; OB = Off-break

This table is dominated by outright speed and spin. On his day Curtly Ambrose has been the most formidable Test bowler of the 1990s, despite a lot more publicity being devoted to Shane Warne. When in the mood, Ambrose may have been even more dangerous than Marshall, but was not as committed all the time, particularly to the domestic first-class game. He is the only man apart from Gibbs to take a hundred Test wickets against two separate countries: England and Australia. With inspired bursts of controlled hostility, no one has been more likely to run through an international batting line-up when it matters. Ambrose's exceptional height, accuracy and extra bounce often leads to comparison with Garner. Of the two Ambrose is the more predatory and difficult to counter on a pitch with uneven bounce. Garner was more even-tempered, deceptive and consistent. Much can be learned from their respective approaches to the wicket.

Ambrose's is brisk and high-kicking, bristling with intent; Garner's almost slow motion as if, like Peter Roebuck said, he was wading through water.

Ian Bishop looked devastating when he first burst on the scene, but serious back injuries have reduced his pace and effectiveness. Courtney Walsh, on the other hand, has appeared physically indestructible. Over after over, year after year, stamina and heart have kept him going – most dangerously when others have given up.

When Imran Khan's powers waned, Pakistan was fortunate that a pair of equally gifted fast bowlers were there to take over. Before the Second World War, left-arm pace bowlers operated from round the wicket. Since then they have generally come over, but they need to be able to swing the ball back to be effective. Otherwise, there is too much the batsman can leave alone or allow to strike his pads. No bowler of this type has switched so easily from one side of the wicket to the other as Wasim Akram. A short run and fast arm action generates late swing and sharp movement, sometimes in opposite directions within the same delivery. Wasim has bowled well in Australia, but less successfully in the Caribbean. His partner Waqar Younis is faster, but more reliant on an old ball for reverse inswing. Waqar's five wickets per Test is the joint highest ratio among current bowlers, and his strike rate is also exceptional. Prone to overpitching in search of extra swing, he is less economical than most. Waqar's record in Australia is poor, and against the stronger batting sides of the 1990s he has not looked quite as formidable as Ambrose.

Waqar's closest rival as fastest bowler of the decade, as well as for wickets per match, is South Africa's Allan Donald. Not naturally aggressive, Donald's considerable pace generates from a shortish run. Irresistible bursts are mixed with occasional periods of waywardness. His 33 wickets in England in 1998 are comfortably the most ever taken in a series here by a South African. Glenn McGrath is tall and slim with a nice high action, and the best fast bowler to come out of Australia since Lillee. He has been a key figure in keeping his country at the top.

Shane Warne broke both legs as a child and spent some time getting around with his arms. This partly explains why he has virtually no run-up, but a tremendously powerful action from shoulder, arm and wrist. No one has spun the ball more, not even Mailey, and Warne bowls nothing like the same proportion of loose deliveries. With a lowish arm and mean trajectory, his leg-break generates considerable spin-swerve in the opposite direction, which leads to an unusual line of attack outside leg-stump. The flipper pitches short but still fools top players. Warne has the leading average among spinners in this table, but lies behind the top quicker men.

Mushtaq Ahmed favours what he calls his 'wrong one' for variety to trap the unwary, and gives the ball air to tempt them. He has been more successful abroad than Kumble, who pushes the ball through briskly, producing more top-spin and indrift than leg-break. Wrist-spin's revival is the most welcome development of the 1990s.

The Sri Lankan off-break bowler Muralitharan compares favourably with the leading finger-spinners of the past. In 1997 he made more of an impact in the Caribbean than any visiting off-spinner has ever done, with 16 wickets in two Tests, and the same can be said about his efforts in Pakistan. Muralitharan's 16 wickets in just one Test at The Oval in 1998 was a sensational performance, carrying Sri Lanka to an emphatic first win in England. A double-jointed rotating wrist facilitates prodigious turn at the end of a real dropping loop, which makes him difficult to drive. His wickets per match ratio is now superior to Warne's.

Fraser is the one medium-pacer in the table and the one Englishman. Easily the most dependable bowler in his team, he has tended to be overbowled and has spent a lot of time out through injury. His eighteen wickets in the last two Tests against South Africa in 1998 contributed just as much to England's dramatic turning round of the series as Stewart's match-saving 164 at Old Trafford or Atherton's brave taming of Donald at Trent Bridge. The tense 23-run rubber-sealing victory at Headingley produced a public euphoria last matched after the stirring events on the same ground seventeen years before. Why? Because England had not won a five-Test series since Gatting's tour to Australia in 1986-87. We had taken part in fourteen such series in the meantime, drawing two against West Indies and losing the remaining twelve to Australia, West Indies, Pakistan and South Africa.

And despite all the publicity to the contrary, it has not been shortage of runs, or incompetent captaincy and management, which has been the key factor behind England's decline. Simply the lack of an international-class attack.

CONCLUSIONS

The biggest single influence on the balance of power in Test cricket has been top-quality penetrative bowling, particularly in series away from home. Like most top-quality items, it has been relatively scarce, and most Test teams have been stronger in batting than bowling. One great batsman will not win many Test matches on his own. One great bowler will. Compare George Headley for West Indies in the 1930s with Richard Hadlee for New Zealand in the 1980s.

Of all countries' Test histories, Pakistan's is perhaps the most colourful. Some hoped, after the British left in 1947, that the whole of pre-Partition India would combine as one cricket team, in a similar way that the various independent Caribbean and South American states joined together as West Indies. They underestimated the sub-continent's Moslems' intense desire for independence from Hinduism. Since then, Pakistan has suffered many divisions of its own, and become a country of paradoxes. An Islamic democracy courted by the USA, swaying between civilian and military rule; a land where a woman's word in court counts for little, but where a woman has been Prime Minister. Most of the people consider themselves first a Punjabi, a Baluch or a Sindhi; second a Moslem; and third a Pakistani. Hence the lack of unity which has plagued cricket. As Imran Khan said:

> The history of Pakistan cricket is one of nepotism, inefficiency, corruption and constant bickering. It is also the story of players who have risen above the mire. A cricketer needs immense talent, belief in himself and sheer luck to survive the political maze of our cricket.

Constant dropping and disciplining of players, captains and officials fosters a climate of mistrust and division, ensuring that no one can possibly hang on to power for long. Remarkably, a nation with over 100 million population has seen a lot of family connections within its cricket teams. But family values are one of Pakistan's strengths. There are no old people's homes there. The fervour of a young insecure nation, practising a different religion from all its cricketing opponents, works both ways. It instills pride and confidence in youthful players, who continue to appear from nowhere and adapt with miraculous immediacy to Test cricket. Skilled leaders, such as Kardar and Imran, managed to channel all that natural aggression profitably. All too often, however, the aggression has been unfocused, much of it flowing self-destructively inwards. Pakistani teams, more than any others, have appeared less than the sum of their parts. This has been particularly true on their travels, where they have not achieved what they should have done.

Pakistan enjoyed the privilege of a world-class bowler, Fazal Mahmood, at the beginning of her Test life. This made her a more formidable proposition than either India or New Zealand during the 1950s. Pakistan's batting improved in the 1960s, but the lack of a decent attack during this and much of the following decade meant that few games were won. Since then, one or more of the fast swingers, Imran, Wasim and Waqar, have given Pakistan the capability of winning anywhere. All three must be considered great bowlers because of the number of wickets they took on different types of surface.

The independence of the cooler north-west and north-east areas of the sub-continent deprived India of her most likely supply of fast bowlers. Sweltering heat and slow pitches fashioned a reliance on spin, which was lovely to watch and good for the game. At home it often proved effective; elsewhere a serious limitation. The Indians are nothing like as bellicose as most of their opponents, and this has something to do with their religion. Unlike the linear view of history espoused by the western philosophies of Judeaism, Christianity, and also Islam, eastern religions, such as Hinduism, believe that events move in cycles. Reincarnation is a well-known example. This encourages an easy-going, fatalistic outlook. All things must pass. Our turn will come. Sunil Gavaskar said that he knew he would be Ian Botham's hundredth Test victim. And he was. Actions tend to follow dominant thoughts. The virtue of patience helps save Test matches, but to win them you need to make things happen. Get people out. India seems to believe that victories abroad are not to be. She has not lost a home rubber for eleven years, but during that time has won just one match away – in neighbouring Sri Lanka. Overall, India has failed the acid test of bowling sides out abroad. Her spinners have won a few games, but not enough. The best career average of all the Indian bowlers to take a hundred Test wickets is the 28 of Bedi and Kumble. India's great players are confined to her batsmen: Merchant, Gavaskar, Tendulkar.

Sri Lanka, formerly Ceylon, had been producing entertaining batsmen for fifty years before gaining admittance to the Test arena. In steamy

Colombo, several teams passing through got a decent game. Had Ceylonese players been allowed to represent India, as Rhodesia's did South Africa, a few batsmen would have made their mark at Test level, but hardly any bowlers.

New Zealand's standards of sportsmanship on the cricket field have probably been highest of all. Generally well led, her teams have given the distinct impression that winning cricket matches is not the most important thing in the world. Perhaps producing the world's finest rugby team and a succession of outstanding middle-distance runners has proved enough to outsiders, not to mention the first man to climb Everest. The other face of the coin is that New Zealand cricket has lacked ambition, and there is probably not enough genuine interest within the country to do much about it. New Zealand was amongst the strongest sides only during the 1980s, when Richard Hadlee was capable of bowling anyone out, and Martin Crowe was as good a bat as anyone in the oppostion. Had the Kiwis played more Tests in the 1940s, with Cowie and Donnelly available, they might have developed a comparable team.

The various cricketing nation states of the West Indies draw on a total population of under 6 million: one third of Australia's, one tenth of the UK and less than 1% of India. But street names will show that nowhere else in the world are such a large proportion of famous people cricketers. Public support has been exceptional, notwithstanding the rivalry between the various cricketing centres, and the political differences between black and Indian communities.

Since the last war West Indian sides have never been short of batting. The first time their bowling compared was in the 1960s, and this made them world champions, at last breaking Australia's and England's alternate hold on power. It was also the time when a regular black captain was first installed, and the Caribbean states gained political independence. For a few years the bowling disappeared, and batsmen in opposing teams licked their lips at the prospect of a trip to the sunny islands, where pitches were slowing down. When the Packer affair ended in 1979, West Indies emerged as by far the strongest side, with a full-time Australian physiotherapist, and a harder, more ruthless approach to replace the old calypso spirit. The batting was still formidable, the attack in a class of its own, backed by consistently brilliant fielding. That West Indies went fifteen years without losing a series was down more than anything to the various four-man pace attacks. For constancy of threat, and the ability to extract life and bounce out of the most sluggish pitch, there have been no greater fast bowlers than Marshall, Garner, Holding and Ambrose. The superhuman efforts of these men won many more games for West Indies than the batting genius of Headley, Sobers, Richards or Lara.

South Africa began her international cricket career back in the nineteenth century, but took a long time to find her feet. The first significant breakthrough was winning a first Test and rubber in England in 1935. For the next fifteen years, half of which were lost to war, South Africa possessed one of her most formidable batting line-ups, but did not win a single match. Further evidence of where the real power in Test cricket lies. During the 1950s the South Africans' fielding surpassed even Australia's, and at last they had bowlers to trouble Test batsmen on all wickets: outstanding off-spinner Tayfield and injury-prone quickie Adcock. Series were shared with England and Australia. During the latter half of the following decade they beat them both, and became world champions, succeeding West Indies whom they still could not play because of apartheid. In 1970, growing political pressure to do something about apartheid forced South Africa out of international cricket at her peak, along with great players Barry Richards, Graeme Pollock and Mike Procter, who would shortly have been joined by Vintcent van der Bijl, the man with the best first-class career bowling average (16) anywhere in the world during the past thirty years. Since returning after a 22 year absence in 1992, South African batting has been lacking in class, yet the freshly-named Proteas have been one of the most successful sides. Fielding has again been a strong point, as has the fast bowling of Allan Donald, who is the most notable example of the game spreading from the English-speaking population to the Afrikaaner. With the black and Indian communities taking the game to their hearts, the future looks rosy for South African cricket.

When known as Rhodesia, Zimbabwe was regarded as part of cricketing South Africa, sharing some of its history, so is not a total novice to the international scene. The small population is a drawback, but the Zimbabweans do not look out of their depth.

Since Test cricket began in 1877, Australia has more often than any other country been unofficial world champions. By my calculation 52 years out of 121. The enduring characteristics of Australian cricket are a tough, uncompromising approach, abrasive self-confidence, real teamwork, and an unparalleled will to win. Australian sides tend to wrench most from their resources. The key factor has been Australian bowling. It has been noted that Test teams are normally stronger in batting than bowling. With Australia it has usually been the other way round. During the first twenty years of Test matches, the difference between England's and Australia's batting strength was considerable, even allowing for the fact that many leading English amateurs rarely toured. To start with, Australia's bowling and fielding were sufficiently superior to produce an even balance of power, and to ensure vital public interest. When England's bowling caught up in the mid-1880s, the Mother Country enjoyed a period of ascendancy. It took until the late 1890s for the Aussies' batting to develop fully, and the Edwardian era saw the teams fairly evenly matched.

The three great pre-1914 Australian bowlers were Spofforth, Turner and Trumble. After Trumble retired in 1904 the attack was a bit thin. Immediately after both World Wars, the Australians enjoyed a monopoly of penetrative bowling and carried all before them. But their greatest performer came from the period in between. Leg-spinner Bill O'Reilly towers over the inter-war period, no less than Bradman with the bat. On pitches tailor-made for batsmen, O'Reilly was the one man who consistently bowled them out, in both Test and other first-class cricket, and gets my vote for the best bowler of all time. Partner Grimmett, another leggie, was also high-class. The immediate post-World War Two generation still remembers Ray Lindwall as the ideal fast bowler. When he faded, his mantle at the head of the attack was assumed by quality left-armer Alan Davidson. In the 1970s and early 1980s Dennis Lillee probably surpassed them both.

The Packer Revolution was born in Australia and hit her cricket hardest, a relatively lean dozen years ensuing before the revival of the current decade. Shane Warne is that precious rarity, a match-winning spinner on all wickets, and McGrath as good a fast bowler as any in the world today. Australia are back on top, despite a long-standing inability to compete on the slow turning pitches of the Indian sub-continent.

Even when champions, Australia has not always possessed the very best batsmen. But there is always the feeling that someone will come off. And they usually do, at a briskish rate. Trumper, Macartney and Bradman were all great players. So too McCabe. And from more recent times, Greg Chappell.

And so to England. Where cricket began. And where it developed into a sophisticated game during the eighteenth and nineteenth centuries. The notion of formal competition was crystalised by the first Test matches in 1877, and after a few early shocks English cricket retained its supremacy throughout most of the remainder of the nineteenth century. By the turn of the twentieth, Australia had caught up. A decade of see-sawing followed, before England, with Hobbs and Barnes at the peak of their considerable powers, reached the First World War stronger than ever. After that numbing conflict, things were never the same again. Britain assumed a more modest place in the world. And England's long periods of cricketing hegemony were virtually over. There were further series triumphs of course, but the only prolonged period when England ruled the waves was during the 1950s; when eight years went by without the loss of a rubber. Tellingly, this was also the only time when England's bowling was stronger than her batting. For another twenty years the weaker teams were seen off easily enough. Then as standards evened up around the globe, England became one of the weaker teams.

Whatever the papers may say, there has rarely been much wrong with England's batting, except for a vulnerable period during the 1980s. After both World Wars England was dominated by Australia, and described as weak. Take a look at the batting in those sides. On both occasions it was stronger than today. And during the current decade England has often fielded five batsmen with Test averages around forty.

Looking back through the ages, Grace, Hobbs and Ranjitsinhji (a cricketing Englishman through and through) stand at the highest pinnacle of batsmanship; without weakness. Against any type of bowling, on any pitch, one would back them to make a score. Add Hammond, Hutton and Compton and you have an all-time top six no other country can match.

It is bowling which has usually let England down. At the highest level, bowlers have to be judged by consistent excellence and cutting edge on all wickets, and for my money the greatest English bowlers have been Lohmann, Richardson and Barnes, who are all pre-First World War. Between the wars nobody made a real mark on more than one Ashes series. A number of gifted performers competed for places in the 1950s, not all of whom lasted the distance. The best were Bedser, who touched the heights after a unproductive early career; Laker, typical of English finger-spinners in that he was so much more effective at home than on truer pitches overseas; and, spilling into the next decade, Trueman, who on his day was almost as good as he says he was. There has been no one quite in the same class since, and Englishmen have spent an increasing amount of time chasing leather, particularly abroad. During the last thirty years, fifteen bowlers from five different countries have taken a hundred Test wickets at less than twenty five runs apiece. Not one of them is English.

Standards in the English domestic game are no worse than they were. If anything, overseas players have raised them. County cricket used to fill the long gaps between meaningful international matches. Now there are no such gaps, and the championship has become a side show, apart from the very last week of the season.

In English cricket there is a sentimentality which is sometimes mistaken for softness. England has a much longer history, both cricketing and otherwise, than her opponents, and subconsciously feels less to prove. A perverse satisfaction endures when gazing back at defeats of long ago. An old man who saw Bradman's or, better still, Armstrong's Australians will find a keener audience than one waxing lyrical over a Hammond double hundred. Who are England's cricketing heroes of the 1990s? Shane Warne and Brian Lara. There is nothing wrong with this. The biggest barrier to true enjoyment of any sport is partisanship. And there is so much in cricket to appreciate, no matter who wins.

If bowlers create most of the opportunities to win Test matches, they still need support. A few years ago I wrote an article for *Cricket Lore* entitled *Fielding: Cricket's Unsung Art*. Fielding, including wicket-keeping, has always played a vital part in winning games of cricket, but it is largely ignored by the media, and hence the public. A run saved is a run made, as they used to say, and a missed chance gives bowlers one more wicket to take. It is difficult enough to take twenty wickets in a Test match.

The southern hemisphere countries, Australia, South Africa, New Zealand, and now Zimbabwe, have generally fielded best. All four boast strong rugby traditions, with emphasis on fitness and teamwork. Their inhabitants also spend more time out of doors than the variable British climate allows. Australia's belief in youth over experience has been another important factor, as has her involvement with baseball. The growth of one-day cricket helped England and West Indies catch up in the late 1970s, and the outstanding West Indian team of the early 1980s surpassed allcomers. General fielding standards during the past twenty years have been higher than ever before, and there are more outstanding bowlers around to take advantage.

The most accomplished fielding sides operate as a unit, making the batsman feel he is in the middle of a giant clam, opening and closing on him. In Test cricket the three most important positions are those of wicket-keeper, first and second slips. A high proportion of catches fly off the outside edge. With no quantitative measures available other than catches taken, identifying outstanding fielders relies on qualitative judgements, including one's own. Leaving wicket-keepers aside for the moment, the first great Australian fielder was tiny Syd Gregory in the covers, his lightning speed and return illuminating a Test career spanning twenty-two years to 1912. Cousin Jack's anticipation and reach at first slip featured strongly in Armstrong's side after the First World War, which veteran Wisden editor Sydney Pardon did not hesitate to proclaim the best fielding team he had seen. There is a striking photograph in David Frith's pictorial history *England v Australia* of Jack Gregory moving behind the wicket-keeper to the leg side, having just spotted Mailey's googly. Another star of Armstrong's team was 'Nip' Pellew in the outfield.

The greatest Australian fielder of the inter-war period was Victor Richardson in various positions on the off side. No one could ever remember his enormous hands spilling a catch, and he ran out more batsmen in Australia than anyone before the Second World War. Neil Harvey is probably the most highly rated all-round fieldsman from his country; Bobby Simpson the best slip catcher from anywhere. Simpson stood wider than most and picked up virtually everything with two hands. O'Neill (outfield) and Davidson (short-leg) were also outstanding. So too Greg Chappell (a grandson of Victor Richardson) in the slips or elsewhere, and now Mark Waugh.

South Africa has produced great outfielders in Owen-Smith, Bland and Jonty Rhodes. No one has equalled Bland's ability to hit the stumps from any angle, and few have approached Rhodes' speed to the ball. The South Africans' fielding during the 1950s brought widespread admiration, Russell Endean being the shining light, either close catching or further out. He also kept wicket on occasions. New Zealand's fielding has been consistently good, as it has usually needed to be, without any one individual really standing out. Martin Donnelly was pretty sharp both in the covers and the leg trap.

English teams may not often have led the world for prowess in the field, but they have thrown up individuals to rank with the best. EM Grace, WG's elder brother, was the acknowledged expert at old-fashioned point, a few yards square of the batsman on the off side. It was really a position for the false stroke on uneven turf. When pitches improved around the turn of the century, point was replaced by the new position of 'gully', invented for mistimed cuts and thick edges by AO Jones of Nottinghamshire. Jones is one of England's two greatest all-round fieldsmen, along with Percy Chapman. Hammond and Lohmann have been our leading slips, while Jessop, Hobbs and Randall stand out among English cover fieldsmen. Each had their own particular style. Jessop stood deeper than most because his throw was so powerful; Hobbs appeared to labour towards the ball before suddenly accelerating and whipping it in, fooling many; Randall, on the other hand, actually ran in as the bowler approached, visibly lifting teammates and crowd. Tony Lock was the most brilliant of the many short-legs springing up in the 1950s to support all the off-spinners and inswingers, and there has never been a more spectacular catcher off his own bowling.

The greatest all-round fielder of all time was the Trinidadian Learie Constantine. Some of his close catches would never have been taken by anyone else, because no one else would have had the audacity to instruct the bowler to feed a batsman's favourite stroke so that the full-blooded hit could be picked up as soon as it left the bat. In the outfield he was never still. Constantine's philosophy was that a fielder should make catches, not just wait for them to come along. CLR James quotes an amazing example:

> George Gunn brought to the West Indies his habit of walking down the pitch to meet the ball just as it pitched. He did this once. The second time as he started to go down Constantine, at second slip, moved fast and began walking side by side with him: Gunn did not completely control the stroke: he edged the ball slightly, the catch was a dolly and Constantine picked it up one-handed. I presume that such a repsonse to his adventurous habits had never happened to Gunn before. That alertness was behind many of the catches.

The four outstanding fielders in the dominant West Indian side of the 1980s were Harper, Logie, Richards and Lloyd. Lloyd had retired to the slips, having earlier prowled the covers. Harper's lightning pick-up and throw from the bowling crease to run out Gooch, as the latter played a quick-footed drive in the Lord's Bicentenary match of 1987, will long be remembered. Fielding standards have been lowest on the Indian sub-continent, where the climate is less conducive to prolonged physical exertion, and dropped catches have cost both India and Pakistan dearly.

One measure which can be applied to close fielders is catches per match, and in Test cricket the results are instructive. Taking a minimum of fifty catches, only two men manage a ratio in excess of one and a half catches per match. One is predictably Bobby Simpson with 1.77 per Test, which excludes a further catch taken as substitute. The clear leader is short-leg specialist Eknath Solkar of India, with a stunning 1.96 catches per game. Solkar's exceptional catching had a lot to do with India's successes in the 1970s. Like Lock, he was always looking to move forward, terrorising batsmen already unsure of where to move their feet to the Indian spinners. Learie Constantine did not play enough Tests to take fifty catches, but did manage 28 in 18 games – a ratio of 1.55. He also spent a fair amount of time in the outfield.

Fifty years ago, an objective exercise to identify the greatest wicket-keeper of all time would have finished up as a straight fight between three Australians, Blackham, Oldfield and Tallon, who respectively represented:

pioneering dexterity; neat artistry; and glove speed. Since then the outstanding keepers, with one exception, have been English: Godfrey Evans, unsurpassed at standing up to medium-fast bowling; Alan Knott, who preferred to stand back to it; and Bob Taylor, a model of technique. The exception was Pakistan's Wasim Bari, whom Knott considered the best all-round keeper in the game at the time. Of these seven masters, only Knott averaged thirty with the bat in Test cricket. He is also the sole full-time wicket-keeper to qualify for any of my batting tables. Since he retired, selectors everywhere have increasingly made the expensive mistake of treating specialist work behind the stumps as less important than a few extra runs in the late-middle order.

In an article for *The Journal of The Cricket Society*, I once looked at how many all-rounders had contributed significantly with both bat and ball in Test cricket. Taking Test history in its entirety, the average number of runs scored per wicket lost is around thirty. I decided to identify those players who had averaged thirty with the bat, and had captured their wickets at a cost below that figure. Applying a minimum qualification of 1000 runs and 100 wickets, only seven men have achieved this in over 120 years. There are two Englishmen – Rhodes and Botham; two Australians – Noble and Miller; one South African – Goddard; one Indian – Kapil Dev; and one Pakistani – Imran Khan. Nobody features from West Indies. Sobers' bowling was too expensive. What about WG? His first-class wickets are numbered in thousands, but only nine came in Test matches.

The batting tables in this book show a line drawn at a point one and a third times the average runs per wicket – to reflect the fact that the main batsmen are expected to score higher than average to make up for the tail. An average runs per wicket of thirty brings a "batting norm" of forty. Not one of the seven all-rounders just identified averaged forty with the bat in Tests. And nobody appears above the line in both my batting and bowling tables. I believe this proves that at Test level there has never been anyone in the top class as both batsman and bowler.

When success proves elusive in international cricket, the usual scapegoat is the captain, rather than the manager as in football. But how much difference can a Test captain really make? The answer is some. But he cannot turn a bunch of losers into world-beaters. Only a great bowler can do that. The next question is how many captains have actually made a significant difference through their leadership alone. Not many. For England one can pick out Illingworth and Brearley, and, in his own way, Jardine. Illingworth retained vast banks of knowledge, with a Don Revie-like mental dossier on every opponent. He was very tactically astute and an excellent reader of pitches. He also had a temper and did not like to give way in an argument. Brearley, on the other hand, was calmness personified, and a formidable psychologist. With him at the helm, England always seemed to be in control even when they shouldn't have been. Jardine was an imposing figure who secured the unswerving loyalty of most of his charges, but his inflexibility made it inevitable that his time in the job would be short.

Australia has produced most outstanding captains. Warwick Armstrong enjoys one of the most impressive records, but he presided over mainly one-sided contests, concentrating as much as anything on winding up the opposition. Noble was a more intelligent leader, the first regularly to set different fields for different batsmen. His captaincy played an important part in beating a theoretically stronger England in 1909. It is easy to say that Bradman's task was straightforward because he had his own batting and a frequent monopoly of penetrative bowling. Anyone picking up his instructional book, *The Art of Cricket*, will quickly realise how deeply he understood the game. No one was quicker to spot opponents' weaknesses. Television watchers will be familiar with Richie Benaud's perceptiveness and uncanny ability to anticipate events. Under his leadership Australia won five successive series between 1958 and 1961, when they often did not have the best players. His last rubber in charge was drawn, when he gave nothing away to more talented opponents.

Ian Chappell was a hard man who dragged Australian cricket up by its bootlaces during the first half of the 1970s. Contemptuous of authority and opponents alike, he extracted the best out of his tough team and ensured that it was feared, in particular for the ruthless short-pitched attack of Lillee and Thomson. Mark Taylor is a more easy-going soul, which is probably why he takes so much stick from Chappell in the Press Box. But Taylor is an excellent captain. Undeterred by lapses of his own form with the bat, he time and again makes decisions which others question – tosses, follow-ons, bowling and fielding changes – and is nearly always proved right. Taylor exudes the courage of his convictions, and remains the only captain to win a series in the Caribbean since Ian Chappell did so twenty five years ago.

West Indies' great captains were Frank Worrell, whose considerable presence welded men from different nation states into a team, and guided them towards their full potential; and Clive Lloyd, who built the most formidable combination ever to take the cricket field, and ensured that it stayed at the top.

The most able South African Test captains were HG 'Nummy' Deane and Jack Cheetham. Deane's shrewd decision-making in the middle of the inter-war period extended limited resources beyond their perceived capabilities. It would have been interesting to see him in charge of a stronger side. Cheetham in the 1950s was more of a motivator, fighting to banish the South Africans' inferiority complex; urging them to compete all the way and to field better than any side had done to that time. Clive Rice's vibrant and successful leadership of Transvaal and Nottinghamshire suggests that he might well have turned out to be South Africa's outstanding captain, had he had the chance.

New Zealand captains have generally been pretty competent, bearing in mind that they have not often had a lot to play with. None demands to be placed above the rest. And no out of the ordinary leader springs to mind from India, Sri Lanka or new boys Zimbabwe. Indian skippers tend to be on the cautious side.

Abdul Hafeez Kardar's patriotic, driving style brought Pakistan's first teams of mainly honest journeymen better results than anyone expected. Far more talented Pakistani sides have achieved less. As soon as a man takes charge in Pakistan, he is looking over his shoulder to see where the next coup is coming from. Imran Khan was big enough not to want the captaincy that badly, nor once in command to worry about losing it. He could be aloof, arrogant even, but a determination to stand above dissent and intrigue made up for occasional tactical lapses. Most important, the Pakistani dressing room listened to him. When he threatened that the first man to back away from fast bowling would be on the next flight home, they knew he meant business and responded. Imran made a success of perhaps the most difficult job in sport. He was the first Pakistan captain to win series in India and England. General Zia knew what he was doing when ordering Imran to take the side to the West Indies, Pakistan coming within a whisker of another historic triumph.

Because Test cricket is the ultimate test, it will be secure for the foreseeable future, certainly in this country. Do not believe all the scaremongers who say that unless England gets a winning team together, people will not watch anymore. They are the kind of pessimists who will tell you at the end of May that in three weeks time the nights will be drawing in. England has not been a leading cricketing power for a generation, yet a full house at Test matches remains more or less guaranteed. Then there are the millions watching on television. Sky would not be paying what they are for TV rights if there was no product.

The time has probably come to satisfy the modern fetish for measuring and ranking everything. Something along the lines proposed by *Wisden* looks sensible, where the result of the last home and away rubbers between any two countries count towards a rolling league table. Teams would have to play every opponent, home and away, say every five years, if only in a one-off match.

Test cricket is still a great game, virtually immune from fluke. To become the world's leading power has always taken a lot of doing. And it always will.

SELECT BIBLIOGRAPHY

Books

HS Altham, *A History of Cricket* (George Allen & Unwin, 1926)

John Arlott, *Rothmans Jubilee History of Cricket 1890-1965* (Arthur Barker, 1965)

Association of Cricket Statisticians and Historians, *Important Cricket Matches 1801-1863* (ACS, eight volumes to 1996)

Ralph Barker and Irving Rosenwater, *England v Australia* (Batsford, 1969)

BCCI, *Forty-Five Years of Ranji Trophy* (BCCI, 1980)

Alec Bedser, *Cricket Choice* (Pelham, 1981)

Donald Bradman, *The Art of Cricket* (Hodder & Stoughton, 1958)

RT Brittenden, *New Zealand Cricketers* (Reed, 1961)

Gerald Brodribb, *All Round The Wicket* (Sporting Handbooks, 1951)

Gerald Brodribb, *Next Man In* (Souvenir Press, 1995)

Graham Dawson and Charlie Wat, *Test Cricket Lists* (Five Mile Press, 1996)

Louis Duffus, *South African Cricket 1927-1947* (South African Cricket Association, 1947)

Bill Frindall, *The Wisden Book of Cricket Records* (Queen Anne Press, 1981)

Bill Frindall, *The Wisden Book of Test Cricket* (Macdonald/Queen Anne Press, 1990)

David Frith, *England versus Australia: A Pictorial History* (Lutterworth, 1977)

David Frith, *The Fast Men* (Corgi, 1977)

Kenneth Gregory ed, *In Celebration of Cricket* (Granada, 1978)

Arthur Haygarth, *Cricket Scores and Biographies* (Lillywhite, 1862)

Ray Illingworth, *One-Man Committee* (Headline, 1996)

Imran Khan, *All Round View* (Chatto and Windus, 1988)

CLR James, *Beyond A Boundary* (Hutchinson, 1963)

Derek Lodge, *Figures On The Green* (George Allen & Unwin, 1982)

Christopher Martin-Jenkins, *The Complete Who's Who of Test Cricketers* (Orbis, 1980)

AG Moyes, *Australian Batsmen* (Harrap, 1954)
AG Moyes, *Australian Bowlers* (Harrap, 1953)
Christopher Nicole, *West Indian Cricket* (Phoenix, 1957)
Jack Pollard, *Australian Cricket* (Hodder & Stoughton, 1982)
NS Ramaswani, *Indian Cricket* (Shakti Malik, 1976)
KS Ranjitsinhji, *The Jubilee Book of Cricket* (Nelson, 1897)
Shuja ud-din, *Babes of Cricket to World Champion* (Obtainable from
    Martin Wood, 1996)
EW Swanton, *A History of Cricket Volume II* (George Allen & Unwin, 1962)
EW Swanton ed, *Barclays World of Cricket* (Collins, 1980)
Pelham Warner, *The Book of Cricket* (Sporting Handbooks, 1945)
Simon Wilde, *Letting Rip* (Witherby, 1994)
Wisden Cricketers Almanack (1864 to the present day)
Peter Wynne-Thomas, *Cricket Records* (Hamlyn, 1983)
Peter Wynne-Thomas, *The History of Cricket* (The Stationery Office, 1997)

Periodicals and Journals

Cricket Lore
The Cricketer
*The Cricket Statistician (and various other publications by the Association of
    Cricket Statisticians and Historians)*
The Journal of The Cricket Society
Wisden Cricket Monthly

INDEX